BIG BOOK OF BBQ

from the editors of
Southern Living

ISBN-13: 978-0-8487-3332-2
ISBN-10: 0-8487-3332-0
Library of Congress Control Number: 2009937172

Printed in the United States of America
Third Printing 2012

Oxmoor House, Inc.

VP, Publishing Director: Jim Childs
Editorial Director: Susan Payne Dobbs
Brand Manager: Daniel Fagan
Senior Editor: Rebecca Brennan

Southern Living Big Book of BBQ

Project Editor: Vanessa Lynn Rusch
Senior Designer: Emily Albright Parrish
Director, Test Kitchens: Elizabeth Tyler Austin
Assistant Director, Test Kitchens: Julie Christopher
Test Kitchens Professionals: Allison E. Cox, Julie Gunter,
    Kathleen Royal Phillips, Catherine Crowell Steele
Photography Director: Jim Bathie
Senior Photographers: Ralph Anderson, Van Chaplin, Gary Clark,
    Jennifer Davick, Art Meripol
Photographers: Robbie Caponetto, Laurey W. Glenn, Beth Dreiling Hontzas
Senior Photo Stylist: Kay E. Clarke, Buffy Hargett
Associate Photo Stylist: Katherine Eckert Coyne
Production Manager: Theresa Beste-Farley

Contributors

Editor: Elizabeth Taliaferro
Barbecue Consultant: Troy Black
Writers: Deborah Garrison Lowery, Ashley T. Strickland
Copy Editor: Donna Baldone
Proofreader: Rhonda Richards
Indexer: Mary Ann Laurens
Interns: Wendy Ball, Chris Cosgrove, Georgia Dodge, Allison Sperando,
    Christine Taylor
Food Stylists: Alyson Haynes, Margaret Dickey
Photographers: Noel Barnhurst, Dan Brant, Charlie Brown, Lisa Romerein,
    Charles Walton IV

To order additional publications, call 1-800-765-6400 or 1-800-491-0551

For more books to enrich your life, visit **oxmoorhouse.com**
To search, savor, and share thousands of recipes, visit **myrecipes.com**

Cover: Cider Vinegar Barbecue Sauce and pulled pork (page 170),
Roasted Camp Corn (page 258), Troy's Baby Back Ribs (page 60)

BIG BOOK of BBQ

Recipes and Revelations From the Barbecue Belt

Oxmoor House®

contents

pit master's welcome

"Whatever you have in your backyard, you probably have something that can be used to produce great barbecue." — Troy Black

Barbecue, Barbeque, BBQ, Bar-B-Q,

or just Q—no matter how you spell it—barbecue is not just a type of cuisine. I like to think of it as a food group all its own. And the word barbecue is an event as much as a type of food; it's an all-day or all-night cookfest with friends. For me, barbecue is a labor of love. It's not only the cooking; it's everything that goes along with it. It's hanging out in the backyard with friends sipping on beers. It's trying to outdo your last attempt at the perfect ribs. It's trying out a new flavor. It's making your neighbor go, "WOW!"

As I travel the country competing in more than 30 professional barbecue contests a year, teaching the art and techniques of low and slow smoking and eating my way through vastly different interpretations of what is called barbecue, it's evident that no matter where they live, people have a strong passion for barbecue. The growth explosion of the barbecue industry the past few years is no surprise. More people are cooking at home. Technology has given us new tools to master the grill. The grocery aisles are filled with sauces, dry rubs, and marinades. Even the number of barbecue competitions is on the rise.

Each year, there are more than 500 sanctioned barbecue contests in the United States. That's right, I said sanctioned! Just like NASCAR, Bassmasters, and other professional sports, there are sanctioning organizations for barbecue competitions. These cook-offs attract more than 8,000 pit masters each year. These guys and gals compete for thousands of dollars each weekend and travel hundreds, even thousands of miles to chase the title of Grand Champion. Some of these teams have more invested in their BBQ rigs than they do in their houses!

Growing up in Athens, Alabama, my favorite local barbecue joint was Whitt's Barbecue. It was a simple, drive-thru-only shack with a limited menu. A barbecue sandwich consisted of succulent pulled pork, vinegar-based slaw, a sliced pickle, and mayonnaise. As a kid, I never knew that you could create pulled pork like that at home.

As an adult, I wasn't satisfied with the local barbecue joints, so I began a quest to create great 'cue myself. I experimented with all kinds of grills and smokers, seasonings, sauces, and techniques. I made lots of mistakes. Some of what came off the grill had to go straight into the trash. I even sacrilegiously boiled ribs a few times until I figured out how to get them tender on the smoker. After a burning desire (pun intended) and lots of patience, I began to understand key elements in producing tender, slow-smoked meats, and I realized that meats could be slow-smoked on just about any kind of backyard cooker. The key was being able to maintain the temperature low enough to cook low and slow. Today there are lots of types of grills and dedicated smokers that make it easy to cook low and slow. Whatever you have in your backyard, you probably have something that can be used to produce great barbecue.

I'm proud and excited about *Southern Living* Big Book of BBQ. This collection of recipes represents some of the best flavors, techniques, and tips that'll help you master the art of great 'cue and become the envy of your neighborhood!

Troy Black competes full-time on the professional barbecue circuit and conducts barbecue schools nationwide. He has won 9 state BBQ titles and consistently finishes in the top 10.

OWENSBORO

BAR-B-Q CAPITAL
OF THE WORLD

KENTUCKY

THE PINK PIG

BLACK'S BBQ
EST. 1932

TEXAS OLDEST AND BEST
JOR BBQ RESTAURANT
ONTINUOSLY OWNED BY
THE SAME FAMILY

Bubbalou's
Bodacious
BAR-B-QUE

SMOKED
HAMS & TURKEY

The
Pink
Ladies

WILBER'S
BARBECUE

Braggin' rights

barbecue defined

Barbecue lovers may politely tolerate preferences of another region but will defend with religious fervor the 'cue they grew up on. Pride and diversity—they're the beauty of barbecue.

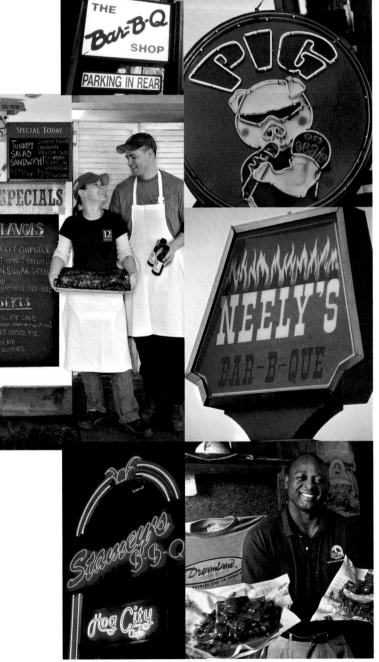

what it is

Barbecue, barbeque, BBQ, Bar-B-Q, 'Cue, "Q," 'Que: (BAR-bah-q) noun: A revered cultural experience in the South involving smoky slow-cooked meat, sauce, sweet tea, friends, family, and lots of laughter

Oddly enough, Southerners have a hard time agreeing about the specifics of what makes "the best" barbecue, yet most find it easy to agree on a few common elements. **First there's the meat.** It's got to be cooked carefully for a long time, usually over an open wood fire.

Then there's the sauce. Which kind to use is the real point of controversy. But without the sauce, it just isn't barbecue. Even if the sauce is sloshed on during cooking or stirred into pulled or chopped meat, you have to serve it on the side at the table so folks can squirt on more.

Next you've got to eat it in a place with atmosphere. Or tradition. Or a collection of pig paraphernalia for decor. With people you like. Where there's enough smoke to stick to your clothes when you leave.

what it isn't

Barbecue (BAR-b-q): verb: A term used improperly by non-Southerners to describe the act of cooking meat (or anything else) on a grill, whether it has a sauce or not.

Any ol' meat on the grill is not real BBQ!

where it is

All Southerners agree on what can be classified as bona fide barbecue, but most disagree on what real barbecue should be. The biggest regional fusses are over meat, sauces, sides, and what to drink with it.

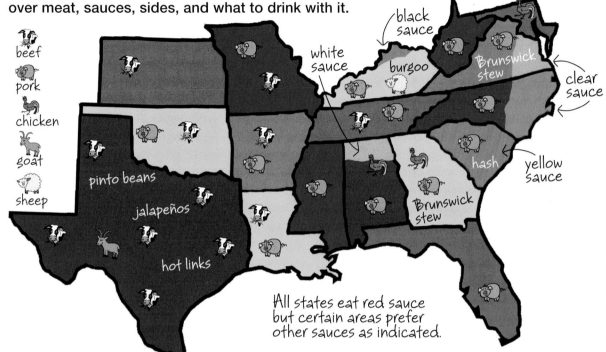

beef
pork
chicken
goat
sheep

pinto beans
jalapeños
hot links

black sauce
white sauce
burgoo
Brunswick stew
clear sauce
hash
yellow sauce
Brunswick stew

All states eat red sauce but certain areas prefer other sauces as indicated.

Meat. There's no disputing that pork is the meat of choice in most areas of the barbecue belt. But Texans will fight for beef (especially brisket) and even goat, northern Kentuckians for mutton, and in Maryland, chicken is king.

Sauces The rainbow of barbecue sauces—with bases of tomato, mustard, mayonnaise, or vinegar— probably provokes the most fighting words. Mustard-style is a favorite in South Carolina, but vinegar–based rules in eastern North Carolina. North Alabama typically serves mayo-based sauce on chicken, and variations of red tomato-based sauces are found all over.

Sides Baked beans, coleslaw, potato salad, fries, corn on the cob, white bread, and hushpuppies are universal for serving with barbecue. But other choices reflect unwritten regional rules. You'll get your Q with liver hash in South Carolina, with Brunswick stew in Georgia and parts of Virginia, or with burgoo in Kentucky. In Texas it comes with hot links (sausage) and jalapeños, and in the Delmarva Peninsula, add a pickle, applesauce, sliced fresh tomatoes, and even collard greens.

Drinks Most everywhere barbecue is served, iced sweet tea is a standard. At big family barbecue events, pitchers of ice-cold lemonade are plentiful too. In Texas the preference in some spots is the locally brewed beer, or in the Hill Country, a tall, cold bottle of Big Red soft drink.

puttin' on the pork

Pork's the favorite meat for barbecue—hooves down. But it's the cook's choice as to the preferred pork part to put on the grill and whether to pull it, chop it, or slice it when it's done.

pickin' parts of the pig

Wondering what pork part makes the best barbecue?
Well, if you're hosting a pig pickin' party (very popular in the Carolinas), pit masters like Josh and Jim Gibson of Beaufort, S.C., (pictured above) use the whole hog cooked over a temporary cinder block pit, which makes it easy for guests to file by and pick the meat right off the pig. Some restaurants choose to cook the whole pig, too, especially those in eastern North Carolina.

Barbecue restaurants that don't cook the whole hogs usually use whole pork shoulders. These are hard to get in supermarkets, so home cooks can use Boston butts (which are half shoulders), pork chops, or ribs to smoke over indirect heat in charcoal smokers or on grills. Warehouse clubs do often carry whole pork shoulders.

Spareribs—the tastiest; country-style ribs—the meatiest; and baby back ribs rubbed with a mixture of spices and mopped with vinegar sauce make the ultimate finger food well worth the mess—and the dry-cleaning bill!

pulled, chopped, or sliced?

If your plateful of barbecue is finely chopped, then it's a good bet you're in North Carolina. Not far away, in Manning, South Carolina, David McCabe, of McCabe's BBQ wouldn't dare chop the meat. "It's so tender when it comes off the pit, it literally falls apart in your hands," says McCabe.

Pulling two forks through the steaming hot meat helps to separate it so you get succulent strands that are crispy and smoked on one end and melt-in-your-mouth tender on the other end. This pulled version also is popular in North Alabama as well as in many other areas around the South.

In Texas you'll find the brisket sliced most often, and occasionally chopped, but sliced pork is offered at some barbecue houses there, too. In fact, you can pretty much count on options being the norm.

Many barbecue joints even let you choose your favorite part of the pig. "Inside meat" is moist and juicy while "outside meat" is drier, smokier-tasting, and brown with crunchy bits of pork skin. Just right for dippin' in sauce!

other meats that matter

Forget pork. The preferred 'cue in some areas today reflects where beef, goat, sheep, chickens, and turkeys were once more prolific than pigs.

beef

Surely you can guess where beef is king on the barbecue plate. Yep, folks, the farther west you go (are ya' thinking Texas and Oklahoma?), the more likely it is that you'll find beef as the 'cue of choice. Sliced is the way it's served in most places, although sometimes it's chopped. And it's always brisket, the tough chest of the cow, which melts into tender heaven during long, low-heat cooking. A plate isn't complete without a couple of beef or pork sausage "hot links" on the side. Sauces are never served on the meat. It's the customer's choice to add that. That's because, they say with typical Texas pride, their barbecued beef is just too good to cover up.

mutton

Barbecued mutton tastes "like an excellent piece of aged beef," says Ken Bosley of Moonlite Bar-B-Q Inn in Owensboro, KY. The long, slow barbecue cooking process suits the tougher meat of mature sheep. Though it's hard to find sheep in Kentucky now, Dutch settlers in the late 1800's had plenty of them and are credited with the mutton preference that exists today.

chicken

These days, chicken barbecue is easy to find almost anywhere. However, in Delaware and Maryland, where chickens outnumber people, it's natural that the 'cue menus are heavy on the winged version. But the question there is: Will that be 'cue with or without bones? Chicken is served pulled off the bone (pork-style) or as the traditional bone-in half- or quarter-chicken, slow-cooked and succulent. During summer months you'll have a chance to savor tender chicken cooked over open-fire pits along highways leading to the coast.

As is tradition, local firefighters, church groups, and civic clubs set up pits and line the road to raise money for causes and offer hot-off-the-fire barbecue chicken—along with must-have sides—to beach-bound travelers.

sauces & sides

In most places, the sauce is as important as the meat. Side dishes rank a close second. Check out this primer on who serves what and where.

sauces

Thick or thin? Red or white? Spicy or not?
Here's the lowdown on sauces and seasoning rubs.

◆**White** Big Bob Gibson Bar-B-Q in Decatur, Alabama, is credited with first serving this creamy mayonnaise-vinegar sauce, sometimes called "Alabama white sauce," with smoked chicken more than 75 years ago.

◆**Yellow** South Carolina takes claim for the sweet-tart golden mustard-style sauce served in the state. It's a sauce South Carolinians have used since the 1700s, when Germans settled there and brought with them their love and heavy use of mustard.

◆**Red** Actually this tomato-based sauce can come in any shade from dark brown to rusty red. No matter the color, it is far and away the most common type of sauce, although historically it came about only after the appearance of ketchup in the early 1900s. Texans love the thick, sweet style on their brisket—if they use a sauce at all.

In Memphis those who love "wet" ribs spread on a sweet tomato sauce. Ketchup and vinegar form the typical base, but colors change with the addition of Worcestershire sauce or chili sauce. The sweetness comes from either brown sugar or molasses.

◆**Clear** Peppery vinegar sauces are mostly used in the coastal areas of North Carolina, South Carolina, Virginia, and Georgia. Red pepper lends the spicy flavor that is the defining factor of famous eastern North Carolina barbecue.

◆**Black** Perhaps least known, except in Kentucky, is the Owensboro black sauce, a traditional blend of vinegar, Worcestershire sauce, and brown sugar, served as a dipping sauce with mutton barbecue.

◆**Rubs** Using a mixture of dry spices rubbed on the meat before cooking forms a bit of a crust that seals in juices and often replaces the sauce. A spicy rub is the secret for famous Memphis "dry" ribs.

sides

Traditional side dishes served with barbecue are just as regionally defined as the meat and the sauce. Although many sides are universal, such as sweet tea and slices of white bread, others are simply local area favorites.

Baked Beans You won't find baked beans at every barbecue affair, but you can count on Texas, Alabama, and Missouri to have them. Most of the South prefers tiny beans, like the ones in the pork and bean cans, seasoned with molasses, ketchup, and spices. But Texans are partial to heartier pinto beans (not sweetened) to eat with onion slices and jalapeños.

Potato Salad It's a standard barbecue salad, but there's no standard recipe. Options include creamy Southern-style with a base of mustard and mayo, mayo-based flavored with sweet pickles, or a version with sliced new potatoes with the skins still intact. In central Texas, vinegary German-style is preferred.

Hush Puppies Standard barbecue fare in North and South Carolina includes these crisp cornmeal nuggets Southerners elsewhere recognize from fish fries.

Coleslaw Cabbage slaw is a definite with barbecue—and for some, a must on top of the meat in a sandwich.

Still, the coleslaw variations are endless. In North Carolina the cabbage is chopped as finely as the meat and uses the same tangy vinegar sauce. In other areas, shredded slaw is sweet and creamy with a mayonnaise base.

Onion Rings or Fries Or maybe both? Barbecue joints almost everywhere offer these crunchy accompaniments as menu options. Crispy fried okra is a frequent 'cue fare as well.

Hot links It's just a Texas thing. Smoked and cooked with the beef brisket are links of spicy beef and pork sausage, a must-have side dish for every hearty barbecue plate.

Brunswick Stew Only in Virginia and Georgia is this camp-style stew standard fare with 'cue. Both states claim the origin of the recipe, chock-full of various meats and vegetables. Georgia's version is a bit more tomatoey.

Burgoo This thick stew of chicken, vegetables, and mutton is the pride of Kentucky.

Hash South Carolinians expect hash over rice with their barbecue, but three distinct styles, ranging from those using liver, beef, or pork, further distinguish regions within the state.

aimin' for top trophy

The road to a world-class barbecue trophy is paved with well-cooked meat, hard labor, lots of sweat, a clever team name, a secret sauce, the favor of 'cue judges, and lots of serious praying.

the serious side of 'cue

Wanna know what it's like in the serious world of barbecue competition? Then make a trip to Memphis in May World Championship Barbecue Contest, considered by cookers and fans alike to be the Super Bowl of Swine, the Granddaddy of Barbecue, the "big dance." Don't let the party animal hats, the raucous laughter and teasing, the outrageous team names, or irreverent characters fool ya'. Veteran Memphis in May participant Bill Bryant of team Pyropigmaniacs sums it up: "When it comes time for cooking, the fun is over, and it's time to get serious," says Bill. "If you start cooking and you're still partying, you're in trouble."

More than 200 teams at each Memphis in May have paid their dues to get to this big league contest. They've already won other sanctioned barbecue events throughout the South and sacrificed half a year's-worth of weekends and a small fortune to earn their spot on Memphis' barbecue mile.

They've spent much longer than that perfecting their technique. One contestant will vehemently swear to smoking with fruit woods—peach or apple—and snubs hickory like it just walked barefoot through The Peabody. Next door the cook loads a smoker with hickory and then squirts apple juice onto his whole hog. "This is all you need for flavor," he says with shrug.

Carefully chosen meat, wood for smoking, sauce, and investment in a grill that cooks the meat just right is all part of the contest. Wayne Booth and his wife, Linda, team up as the Red Hot Smokers and haul along their red smoker. "I rub my grill every now and then like there's a genie in there," Wayne says, patting the red metal and flashing a grin.

here comes the judge

You gotta have a good name. Seriousness gets set aside when teams set out to come up with a creative moniker. It makes the judges and visitors smile, and that's a good thing. Who can keep from grinning when passing by gaudily decorated booths with names such as Pork Fiction, Swine-O-Mite, Squeal Seekers, Smokers Anonymous, Sow Luau, The Bastey Boys, Getting Piggy With It, Notorious P.I.G., Barefoot in the Pork, Pork Me Tender, Tangled up in Cue, Slab Yo Mama BBQ, Serial Grillers, and The Not Ready for Swine Time Porkers. Though not tongue-in-cheek, one all-female group gets attention with their clever name, The Pink Ladies. A pink picket fence and pots of pink tulips make their name visually memorable.

"Hush up! The judges are comin'!" echos throughout the crowd when it's time for business. Whoopin' and hollerin' levels to church whispers and a reverence settles over Tom Lee Park as the judges begin their booth visits. Each spokesperson has just 15 minutes to plead the teams' case to the judge before serving up a taste. "It's a bit of a dance between the judge and the cooker," says MIM-certified judge Bill Gage. "Both are extremely serious and desire to be the very best at what they do."

Judges taste at each booth, while another sample is sent to a panel for a blind evaluation. Sixteen categories, including ribs, shoulder, whole hog, poultry, and seafood, are analyzed by the highly trained MIM-certified judges. The pacin' and prayin' and sweatin' really begin while contestants wait in agony as tension builds to the climax of announcements from the park stage. When the prizes are awarded, it's whoopin', hollerin', and high fives all around for the winners. For the others, there's always next year.

How To BBQ

barbecue like a pro

Long and slow is the name of the game, and two things are crucial: the right temperature and smoke. Here, we tell you how to get both.

indirect cooking is key

Great barbecue is cooked for a long time over low heat (225° to 250°). Anything hotter and you're actually grilling. This gentle indirect cooking method allows the meat to tenderize. A piece of meat that has been properly smoked has a pinkish ring called a "smoke ring" on the outer half-inch or so. It is a much-desired mark of careful, consistent cooking.

Several options exist for fueling your smoker. Some outdoor chefs prefer all-natural lump charcoal (such as Royal Oak brand), but regular all-natural charcoal briquettes (brands such as Kingsford and Royal Oak) work well, too, provided they aren't labeled "Instant Light." Many competitive barbecue teams, such as those who cook at the Memphis in May International Festival, use regular charcoal briquettes for their consistency and predictability.

Before adding charcoal, wood, or meat, the smoker has to be brought to the proper temperature. If you have a charcoal grill, follow our directions (opposite page) to turn it into a smoker. If you own a traditional smoker, don't miss our favorite method (page 24) for maintaining the right temperature for hours without the need to add charcoal and wood.

Wind and cold temperatures can wreak havoc on your cookout, causing the temperature of your smoker to fluctuate. Place the smoker on the downwind side of your house or another large object to help protect it.

STARTING CHARCOAL.

• An easy way to start charcoal is with a chimney. Pour charcoal in the top, stuff newspaper in the bottom, and light the paper. Always set the chimney inside the grill when heating.
• Place an electric starter in the grill, and pile charcoal on top. Plug in the starter, and after a few minutes, you will have enough charcoal ignited to get the rest of it burning.

chimney

electric starter

smoking in a charcoal grill

Step 1 Heat 20 charcoal briquettes until they are a uniform ashy gray color and flames have died down (see "Starting Charcoal," opposite page). Pile the charcoal against one side of the grill.

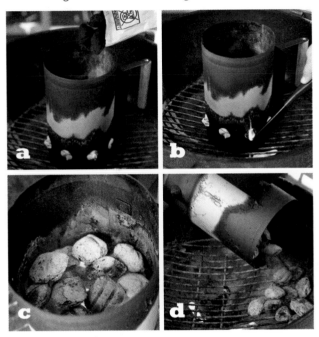

Step 2 Let grill heat, covered with grill lid, at least 10 minutes to get an accurate temperature reading. Optimum smoking temperature should stay between 225° and 250° at all times. If your grill doesn't have a built-in gauge, a thermometer stuck in the top air vent will give an accurate temperature close to the cooking grate (make sure the food to be smoked doesn't touch the probe). Adjust vent openings to achieve desired temperature. To increase the heat, open the vents to give more air to the fire. To decrease, close the vents a little, but be careful not to close them fully.

Step 3 When this temperature range is reached, open the lid; place about 1 cup of drained wood chips that have been soaked in water for at least 30 minutes directly on top of the coals. Place the cooking grate on top; place the item to be smoked in the center of the grate. Close the lid; check the temperature again after 5 minutes. When the correct temperature is reached, the most important step takes place: leaving it alone. This doesn't mean walking away and never looking at it. You'll need to keep an eye on the temperature, adding three or four unlit charcoal briquettes and a handful of wood chips every hour or so.

TEMPERATURE IS KEY

When smoking, the temperature of the meat, not time, is the most important factor in determining doneness. Most smoked meats need to reach higher internal temperatures than other cooked meats. Our recipes tell the recommended temperatures.

using a smoker

A Pit Master's Equipment If you want to invest in a traditional smoker, there are a wide range of prices, sizes, and features to choose from. You'll be able to find the perfect pit for you.

The standard smoker One of the most recognizable smokers is the Weber Smokey Mountain Cooker Smoker. This bullet-shaped smoker is great for those who occasionally slow cook. It costs less than $300 and takes up very little space.

The pit If you do lots of slow smoking, consider a large heavy-duty smoking pit. These pits have several advantages over smaller ones. They keep their temperature for longer periods of time, which means less fire maintenance. They hold more heat, and with proper care, they will last practically forever.

The barrel smoker The barrel-type smoker with an offset firebox has long been a favorite of Texans. The Tejas Smoker Model 2040 is made of heavy-plate steel and has a 20- x 40-inch smoking barrel. A large drain valve makes cleanup easy. The lid opens up on top of the firebox, exposing a grate right above the fire for grilling.

The gas smoker If you like the convenience of a gas grill for your steaks and you like to cook things low and slow, try the All-in-One Grill from Pitts and Spitts. The smoker sports stainless steel construction, a heavy-duty firebox, and an attached gas grill.

WATER OR SAND

Most traditional smokers have pans that are meant to be filled with water. Many believe this is to keep the meat moist while smoking, but the real reason is to help regulate the temperature. Our secret is to fill the water pan with clean sand instead. You can find 50-lb. bags of non-toxic sand in most home-improvement stores for less than $5. This way you won't need to keep refilling the water pan every two to three hours.

The Minion Method There are many ways to set up a smoker, but the method that we love for using a bullet-shaped smoker was developed by Jim Minion from Federal Way, Washington. This is, by far, the easiest and most foolproof one we've seen. It will give constant heat and smoke for 8 to 12 hours.

Step 1 Cut off both ends of a 7- to 8-inch-high can, such as a 3-lb. coffee can, and place it in the center of the charcoal grate. Fill outer ring with charcoal briquettes, and place six to seven large pieces of unsoaked wood on top.

Step 2 Fill can with lit charcoal, and gently remove can with a pair of long metal pliers. (Be sure to wear an oven mitt, because heat will transfer quickly to the metal pliers.) Assemble remaining smoker parts as directed by the manufacturer.

woods for smoking

Some aficionados will tell you only hickory can be used. Others will tell you only oak, only maple, only mesquite . . . and the list goes on. The truth is, most any hardwood will do. Each one will add its own subtle flavor, so we recommend trying all different types before settling on one or a combination of woods. Avoid soft woods, such as pine, cedar, or spruce, which contain resin and tar that may be harmful. If using shredded wood, soak it in water for at least 30 minutes prior to placing on coals. Big chunks of wood can go directly on coals without soaking.

Hickory This undeniable king of smoking woods is wonderful with just about any type of meat and fish.

Oak Another great all-purpose wood that is a little milder than hickory, oak works well with pork and poultry.

Fruitwoods Apple, cherry, peach, and plum woods are more delicate in flavor and make poultry, fish, and pork taste great.

Pecan Less intense than hickory, this wood is good for smoking all types of meat.

Maple This produces a medium-intense smoke, perfect for smoking pork and poultry.

Alder The sweeter flavor of this wood is amazing for smoking fish and chicken breasts.

Walnut Its intense flavor is ideal for beef.

Mesquite This powerful wood can create a bitter flavor if used in excess. We like to throw a handful on the coals when grilling, but we shy away from it when smoking.

Try some of these nontraditional ideas.

Grapevines: Similar to fruitwoods, these produce a mild taste in fish and poultry.

Shredded bourbon barrels Made from oak, shredded bourbon barrels are suitable for any kind of meat and fish.

Shredded wine barrels Also made from oak, this subtle flavor shows up more when used with chicken and fish.

indirect & direct heat

Grilling over indirect heat on a charcoal or gas grill cooks meats low and slow, similar to smoking. Cooking over direct heat is actually grilling. Slather on tangy sauces or high-flavor rubs and seasonings for some tasty "speed barbecuing" over direct heat, a faster alternative to barbecuing for weeknight meals.

indirect grilling

This slower grilling method, with the heat source off to the side, allows the heat to circulate around the food and cook it slowly and evenly. It works best for foods such as roasts, ribs, whole chickens, turkeys, and other large cuts that need to grill 30 minutes or longer. When using the indirect method, we like to place food on the direct heat side briefly to get some browning and those all-important grill marks before moving it to the indirect side to finish cooking.

Using a charcoal grill There are a number of ways to set up a charcoal grill for indirect heat. In all of them, we like to use a drip pan to catch any fat and juices coming from the food. This helps keep your grill clean and reduces flare-ups.

Version 1 Place a drip pan against one side of grill on charcoal grate. Arrange hot coals against other side of grill. Grill food on cooking grate over drip pan. This setup works best when both direct and indirect grilling are needed.

Version 2 Place a drip pan in center of charcoal grate. Arrange hot coals on each side. Some manufacturers make baskets for hot charcoal to help contain it against the sides of the grill. This arrangement is good if you want to have one side of the direct heat at a higher or lower temperature than the other.

Version 3 Place a drip pan in center of charcoal grate. Arrange hot coals completely surrounding drip pan. This method is best when grilling larger items such as whole chickens and turkeys.

Using a gas grill Light all burners according to manufacturer's instructions, turn to high, close lid, and preheat 10 minutes. Adjust outside burners to temperature recommended in recipe. Place food on grate; turn off burners directly beneath food.

Version 1

Version 2

Version 3

direct grilling

With direct heat, food cooks over the heat source. This heat is typically used when food such as burgers, steaks, boneless chicken pieces, fish fillets, and vegetables can be fully cooked in 30 minutes or less. Direct heat is also used to sear meat and to get handsome grill marks.

Using a charcoal grill Spread hot coals in a single layer evenly over charcoal grate. Place cooking grate over coals; cover with grill lid. Preheat at least 10 minutes. Adjust temperature before placing food on grill. (To increase heat, open vents to give more air to the fire. To decrease heat, closed vents a little.)

Using a gas grill Light all burners according to manufacturer's instructions. Turn all burners on high, close lid, and preheat 10 minutes. Place food on cooking grate, and close lid. Adjust burners to temperature recommended in recipe.

HANDS-ON-TEMPERATURE

To determine the approximate temperature of your grill, place your hand, palm side down, 5 inches above the cooking grate, and count the seconds you can comfortably hold it there.
- 7 to 8 seconds = Medium-low (250° to 300°)
- 5 to 6 seconds = Medium (300° to 350°)
- 3 to 4 seconds = Medium-high (350° to 400°)
- 2 seconds or less = High (400° to 450°)

ready for pulled pork

Enjoy it at home. The *Southern Living* Test Kitchen teamed with Pit Master Troy Black to perfect this no-fail method for a traditional Southern favorite.

traditional pulled pork

This barbecue rates as the very best for many people. A special night out at a restaurant doesn't mean going to a fine steak house or a nice seafood place. It means visiting a real barbecue joint where the sweet aroma of woodsmoke fills the air, and a barbecue connoisseur can have pulled pork with their choice of texture—inside meat, outside meat, or half and half.

Every barbecue restaurant has secrets that it won't share, no matter what. So for those of us trying to make pulled pork at home, numerous questions come to mind. What cut of meat do they use? What temperature? How long should it cook? What kind of heat do they use? What do they season it with?

To steer us in the right direction, we turned to Troy Black. Not only did he answer our questions, but he also gave us clear step-by-step instructions on how to successfully make pork barbecue in our own backyards.

First you have to start out with the right cut of meat. Most barbecue restaurants use whole pork shoulders, but they're rarely available in grocery stores. If you find a whole shoulder, use it (photo 1). Otherwise, use a bone-in Boston butt, which is half of the shoulder (the other half being the picnic shoulder). If needed, trim the fatback to about ⅛ inch thick. Sprinkle pork generously with Barbecue Rub (page 60), massaging it into the meat (photo 2). Wrap tightly with plastic wrap, and chill at least 1 hour or up to 8 hours.

Smoking a pork shoulder takes about 1 hour for each pound, so you'll need to get an early start. Prepare your smoker or grill for smoking (see "Barbecue Like a Pro" on page 22) until the temperature reaches 250°. Take the meat out of the refrigerator, and let it stand for 30 to 45 minutes. Having the pork at room temperature is very important because if you put it on the smoker cold, the outer portion will burn while the inside will not thoroughly cook.

photo 1

photo 2

Smoke is one of the main ingredients of good barbecue. Soak hickory wood chips (or any other wood chips used for barbecuing) in water overnight. This prevents them from burning. The chips smolder, producing smoke that flavors the meat during the cooking process. The smoke also lends a pink color to the outer inch or so of the flesh, creating what is called a smoke ring. A handful of wood chips should be added to the fire every hour or so unless you are using the Minion Method (page 24). The more chips you add, the stronger smoke flavor you get.

Place meat, fat side down, on the smoker. Maintain the temperature in the smoker between 225° and 250° (photo 3). Use a pit thermometer for an accurate read. Every time wood chips or charcoal are added, spritz the meat with apple juice from a spray bottle. This will add moisture and a fruity background flavor.

When the internal temperature of the pork reaches 165°, use tongs to remove it from smoker (skewering releases vital juices), and place on heavy-duty aluminum foil. Spritz generously with apple juice, and tightly seal foil around pork. Place meat back on the smoker, and cook until temperature reaches 195° (photo 4). Cooking the meat beyond the USDA guideline of 160° renders out the fat and tenderizes the meat.

Remove the meat from smoker, and let stand for 15 to 30 minutes. Unwrap the foil after it has cooled enough to handle. Remove the bones, which will easily pull away, and then begin pulling, or shredding, the meat with two large forks. Discard any remaining fat.

photo 3

photo 4

brisket 'n' ribs

No need to head to your favorite rib joint to enjoy the ultimate finger food or the king of Texas barbecue. You can serve these mouthwatering delicacies at home, so go ahead and give your favorite barbecue spot some competition.

brisket: a taste of Texas

For most of the South, barbecue means pork, but in Texas, brisket is king. If you've never tried this Southwest favorite, you're missing a treat. Consider this hearty cut the next time you fire up the smoker.

Brisket, which comes from the chest of the cow, requires long, slow cooking to tenderize the meat. Although store-bought briskets in Texas are very large, those found in most grocery stores range in weight from 3 to 7 pounds. You can also purchase them at a wholesale club, where they often range from 12 to 14 pounds. If the brisket is untrimmed, ask your butcher to trim the excess fat, leaving about ⅛ inch on the meat.

Several great recipes begin on page 34, so take your pick of seasonings and techniques there. Just remember this tip: Even though beef is done at 145°, we recommend smoking the meat to between 195° and 205° for maximum tenderness.

SALTING BRISKET A Texas brisket expert follows the time-honored tradition of salting the meat by hand.

SMOKE RING Properly cooked meat has a pinkish ring called a smoke ring on the outer ½-inch or so.

all about ribs

Glossary of Ribs Buying ribs is easy if you know what to look for. Single slab packages allow you to see all sides of the ribs. You want as much meat and as little fat as possible.

Beef ribs have very large bones with lots of meat. Because of their size, they require a long cooking time over indirect heat to ensure tender meat.

Spareribs have the least amount of meat and, because they're less tender than other ribs, may take longer to cook. However, they are considered the most flavorful.

Country-style ribs are so meaty they can be eaten with a knife and fork. These ribs are usually sold in packages of six to eight pieces already cut apart for easy grilling.

Baby back ribs (also called baby loin back ribs) have lots of meat between their short bones. These may cost a bit more per pound than spareribs.

Lose the membrane. As you prepare any rib recipe, be sure to carefully remove the thin membrane on the back of the ribs. This will allow smoke and rubs to penetrate the meat better. Then sprinkle on a seasoning rub.

Rackin' 'em up If your grill or smoker is small but your appetite is hankerin' for ribs, consider purchasing a rib rack that holds slabs of ribs vertically so you can cook more at a time.

Cutting Ribs To easily cut ribs apart, hold rack firmly with tongs and, using a serrated knife, slice between each bone. Looking at the concave side of the slab will give a clear guide as to where the bones are.

Low
and
Slow

Fiesta Brisket

Don't shy away from this slow-cooked, robust brisket because of the long ingredients list—you'll love it.

Prep: 30 min.; **Cook:** 5 min.; **Stand:** 30 min.; **Chill:** 2 hr.; **Soak:** 30 min.; **Grill:** 5 hr.

4 guajillo chiles

4 cups boiling water

½ cup cider vinegar

½ cup low-sodium chicken broth

8 garlic cloves

1 medium onion, chopped

3 fresh thyme sprigs

2 tsp. dried Mexican oregano leaves

1½ tsp. ground cumin

½ tsp. ground cloves

½ tsp. ground allspice

3 tsp. salt, divided

2 tsp. ground pepper

1 (4- to 5-lb.) flat-cut beef brisket

8 cups hickory wood chips

2 large limes, cut into wedges

Garnish: fresh cilantro sprig

Shopping tip: Guajillo chiles and Mexican oregano may be found on the spice aisle of specialty grocery stores or in Mexican markets. Dried oregano may be substituted for Mexican oregano.

1. Cook chiles in a skillet over high heat 5 minutes or until fragrant, turning often. Remove stems and seeds from chiles. Place chiles in a large bowl; add 4 cups boiling water, and let stand 20 minutes. Drain.

2. Process chiles, vinegar, next 8 ingredients, and ¾ tsp. salt in a blender or food processor until smooth, stopping to scrape down sides as needed.

3. Sprinkle pepper and remaining 2¼ tsp. salt over brisket. Place brisket in an extra-large zip-top plastic freezer bag or a large shallow dish. Pour chile mixture over brisket; rub brisket with chile mixture. Seal or cover, and chill 2 to 24 hours.

4. Soak wood chips in water 30 minutes. Prepare gas grill by removing cooking grate from 1 side of grill. Close grill lid; light side of grill without cooking grate, leaving other side unlit. Preheat grill to 250° to 300° (low) heat.

5. Spread 4 cups soaked and drained wood chips on a large sheet of heavy-duty aluminum foil. Cover with another sheet of heavy-duty foil, and fold edges to seal. Poke several holes in top of pouch with a fork. Place pouch directly on lit side of grill. Cover with cooking grate.

6. Remove brisket from marinade, discarding marinade. Place brisket, fat side up, in a 12- x 10-inch disposable foil roasting pan. Place pan on unlit side of grill; cover with grill lid.

7. Grill brisket, maintaining an internal temperature of grill between 250° and 300°, for 1½ hours. Carefully tear open foil pouch with tongs, and add remaining 4 cups soaked and drained wood chips to pouch.

8. Cover with grill lid, and grill, maintaining internal temperature of grill between 250° and 300°, until a meat thermometer inserted into thickest portion of brisket registers 165° (about 1½ hours).

9. Remove brisket from grill. Place brisket on a large sheet of heavy-duty aluminum foil, and pour ½ cup pan drippings over brisket; wrap with foil, sealing edges.

10. Return brisket to unlit side of grill; grill, covered with grill lid, until meat thermometer registers between 195° and 205° (about 2 hours). Remove from grill; let stand 10 minutes. Cut brisket across the grain into thin slices. Squeeze juice from limes over brisket before serving. Garnish, if desired. **Makes** 8 servings.

Oven-Roasted Fiesta Brisket: Prepare recipe as directed through Step 3. Preheat oven to 350°. Remove brisket from marinade, discarding marinade. Wrap brisket with heavy-duty aluminum foil, and place in a jelly-roll pan. Bake 3 hours or until a meat thermometer inserted into thickest portion registers 195° and brisket is very tender. Remove from oven, and let stand 10 minutes. Cut brisket across the grain into thin slices.

Trim excess fat, leaving only about 1/8 inch on the meat.

Place brisket in a zip-top plastic freezer bag, and pour chile mixture over meat. Rub chile mixture into brisket.

35

Beef Brisket With Texas Barbecue Sauce

Slice the brisket and pass the sauce on the side or chop the brisket and drench it with the sauce to make saucy sandwiches.

Prep: 15 min.; **Chill:** 8 hr.; **Grill:** 4 hr.

1 cup vegetable oil

1 cup cider vinegar

¼ cup Worcestershire sauce

1 bay leaf, crumbled

1¼ tsp. seasoned salt

2¼ tsp. pepper

¾ tsp. paprika

1 (3-lb.) beef brisket, trimmed

2 pieces of oak or 2 fruit wood chunks

Texas Barbecue Sauce

1. Combine first 4 ingredients in a shallow dish or large zip-top plastic freezer bag.
2. Combine seasoned salt, pepper, and paprika; rub into brisket. Place brisket in marinade.
3. Cover or seal; chill 8 hours, turning occasionally.
4. Prepare a hot fire by placing 2 pieces of oak or 2 fruit wood chunks at front and back of grill, piling charcoal in the center. Let burn until coals are white.
5. Remove brisket from marinade, discarding marinade. Rake coals to 1 side of grill; place meat on other side. Grill, covered, over indirect heat 3 hours or until a meat thermometer inserted into thickest portion registers 195°, maintaining internal temperature of smoker between 225° and 250°.
6. Brush both sides of brisket with 1 cup Texas Barbecue Sauce; cook 1 hour, basting with sauce. Serve with remaining sauce. **Makes** 6 to 8 servings.

Texas Barbecue Sauce

Prep: 10 min.; **Cook:** 10 min.

2 cups ketchup

½ cup cider vinegar

½ cup Worcestershire sauce

1 small onion, grated

¼ cup butter

1 Tbsp. seasoned salt

1 Tbsp. brown sugar

1½ tsp. chili powder

1½ tsp. pepper

1 small bay leaf

1. Bring all ingredients to a boil in a large saucepan. Reduce heat, and simmer, stirring occasionally, 10 minutes. Remove and discard bay leaf from sauce before serving. **Makes** 3 cups.

Texas-Style Smoked Brisket

Bill and Cheryl Jamison frequent America's best barbecue joints for the most notable regional styles to feature in their books. They give Texas high marks for this recipe.

Prep: 32 min.; **Chill:** 24 hr.; **Soak:** 16 hr.; **Stand:** 1 hr., 40 min.; **Grill:** 3 hr., 30 min.; **Cook:** 1 hr., 35 min.

Brisket:

1 Tbsp. brown sugar

1 Tbsp. smoked paprika

1 Tbsp. freshly ground black pepper

1½ tsp. kosher salt

1½ tsp. onion powder

1 (7-oz.) can chipotle chiles in adobo sauce

1 cup chopped onion

¼ cup cider vinegar

¼ cup Worcestershire sauce

1 (12-oz.) can beer

1 (4½-lb.) flat-cut brisket (about 3 inches thick)

8 hickory wood chunks (about 4 lb.)

2 cups (½-inch) sliced onion

2 Tbsp. pickled jalapeño peppers

Sauce:

1 cup fat-free less-sodium beef broth

2 Tbsp. Worcestershire sauce

1 Tbsp. cider vinegar

1 Tbsp. ketchup

1 Tbsp. pickled jalapeño liquid

1. To prepare brisket, combine the first 5 ingredients. Place 2 Tbsp. sugar mixture in a blender. Set aside remaining sugar mixture.

2. Remove 2 chiles and 2 Tbsp. sauce from can; add to blender. Reserve remaining chiles and sauce for another use. Add 1 cup chopped onion and next 3 ingredients to blender; process until smooth. Combine brisket and chipotle mixture in a 2-gal. zip-top plastic freezer bag; seal. Marinate in refrigerator 24 hours, turning occasionally.

3. Soak wood chunks in water about 16 hours; drain. Remove brisket from bag, discarding marinade. Pat brisket dry, and rub with remaining sugar mixture. Let brisket stand at room temperature for 30 minutes.

4. Remove grill rack; set aside. Prepare grill for indirect grilling, heating one side to medium-low and leaving one side with no heat. Maintain temperature at 250°.

5. Pierce bottom of a disposable aluminum foil pan several times with the tip of a knife. Place pan on heated side of grill; add half of wood chunks to pan. Place another disposable aluminum foil pan (do not pierce pan) on unheated side of grill. Pour 2 cups water in pan. Coat grill rack with cooking spray, and place on grill.

6. Place brisket on grill rack over foil pan on unheated side. Close lid; cook 3½ hours or until a meat thermometer registers 170°. Add additional wood chunks halfway during cooking time.

7. Preheat oven to 250°.

8. Remove brisket from grill. Place sliced onion and jalapeños on a large sheet of heavy-duty aluminum foil. Top with brisket; seal tightly. Place foil-wrapped brisket in a large baking pan. Bake at 250° for 1½ hours or until thermometer registers between 195° and 205°. Remove from oven. Let stand, still wrapped, 1 hour. Unwrap brisket, reserving juices; trim and discard fat. Cut brisket across grain into thin slices.

9. To prepare sauce, finely chop sliced onion and jalapeños; set aside. Place brisket juices in a zip-top plastic freezer bag inside a 2-cup glass measure; let stand 10 minutes (fat will rise to the top). Seal bag; carefully snip off 1 bottom corner of bag. Drain ½ cup drippings into a saucepan, stopping before fat layer reaches opening; discard fat and remaining drippings. Add onion, jalapeños, broth, and remaining ingredients to pan; cook over medium heat 5 minutes or until thoroughly heated. **Makes** 10 servings.

In Texas, barbecue is about the beef—if there's any sauce, it's a thin, spicy pan sauce made from the meat drippings.

Smoked Brisket

Here's a simply seasoned brisket that's quick to the grill. Slice and serve it plain or with your favorite barbecue sauce.

Prep: 5 min.; **Soak:** 1 hr.; **Grill:** 5 hr.

Hickory chunks

2 Tbsp. dried rosemary

2 Tbsp. paprika

2 Tbsp. pepper

2 Tbsp. dried garlic flakes

1 tsp. salt

1 (4-lb.) boneless beef brisket

Favorite barbecue sauce

1. Soak wook chunks in water for at least 1 hour. Prepare charcoal fire in smoker; let burn 15 to 20 minutes.

2. Combine rosemary and next 4 ingredients; rub on brisket.

3. Drain wood chunks, and place on coals. Place water pan in smoker; add water to depth of fill line. Place brisket on lower food grate; cover with smoker lid.

4. Smoke brisket, maintaining internal temperature of smoker between 225° and 250°, until a meat thermometer inserted into thickest portion registers 165° (about 3 hours). Remove brisket from smoker, and wrap in aluminum foil. Return to smoker, and smoke until temperature reaches between 195° and 205° (about 2 hours). Remove and let stand 10 minutes. Slice and serve with favorite barbecue sauce. **Makes** 8 servings.

tips from the pit master

When using charcoal for low and slow cooking, use good quality charcoal briquettes. They burn more consistently and make it easier to control the heat.

Rocket City BBQ

Huntsville, Alabama

WhistleStop features a professional and amateur cook-off, a smokin' country act and fun for the entire family!

What is it?

An exciting family event with the Rocket City BBQ Cook-off, Shade Tree barbecue competition, entertainment, and children's activities.

What is there to do?

• Enter either a professional or amateur barbecue competition
• Listen to live music, from country to rock and roll
• Enjoy the Kid's Zone, a free play area with moon bounce, obstacle course, foam machine, giant slide, and more
• Buy freshly cooked barbecue from award–winning vendors

Who hosts it?

The Alabama Constitution Village Foundation (ACV Foundation) hosts its annual Whistle-Stop Festival each May at the historic Huntsville Depot to raise money for the EarlyWorks Museum Complex.

How do I get more information?

For more information visit www.rocketcitybbq.com or www.TheWhistleStopFestival.com, or call (256) 564-8110.

Photos courtesy of Jenny Jacks Photography

Special Occasion Menu

Serves 8 hungry folks

HERB-CRUSTED PRIME RIB

Garlic Mashed Potatoes, page 249

Steamed asparagus

CRUSTY ROLLS

Praline Bundt Cake, page 262

Herb-Crusted Prime Rib

p: 25 min.; **Soak:** 1 hr.; **Grill:** 4 hr., 45 min.; **Stand:** 15 min.

kory wood chunks

rlic cloves, minced

sp. salt

sp. coarsely ground
er

sp. dried rosemary

. dried thyme

b.) beef rib roast

ups dry red wine

ups red wine vinegar

1. Soak wood chunks in water 1 hour.
2. Combine minced garlic and next 4 ingredients, and rub garlic mixture evenly over beef roast.
3. Stir together dry red wine, red wine vinegar, and olive oil; set wine mixture aside.
4. Prepare charcoal fire in smoker; let burn 15 to 20 minutes.
5. Drain wood chunks, and place on coals. Place water pan in smoker, and add water to just below fill line. Place beef roast in center on lower food rack. Gradually pour wine mixture over beef roast.
6. Cook beef roast, covered, 4 hours and 45 minutes or until a meat thermometer inserted into thickest portion of beef roast registers 145° (medium), adding more water to depth of fill line, if necessary, and keeping temperature between 240° and 250°. Remove beef roast from smoker, and let stand 15 minutes before slicing. **Makes**

Sweet-and-Sour Grilled Ribs

Prep: 15 min.; **Grill:** 2 hr., 30 min.

1 (11.5-oz.) bottle sweet and
sour sauce

⅓ cup pineapple juice

2 garlic cloves, pressed

1 Tbsp. brown sugar

4 lb. beef ribs or spareribs

¼ tsp. salt

Shopping tip: We tested
with Kikkoman Sweet and
Sour Sauce.

1. Stir together first 4 ingredients. Set sauce aside.
2. Prepare a hot fire by piling charcoal or lava rocks on each side of grill, leaving center empty. Place a drip pan in center. Coat food grate with cooking spray, and place on grill.
3. Sprinkle ribs with salt. Arrange ribs on food grate over drip pan. Grill, covered with grill lid, 2½ hours to 3½ hours or until the ribs bend easily, basting with sauce twice during the last hour and keeping temperature between 225° and 250°. **Makes** 4 servings.

Mississippi

Here's where to get great 'Q in the state.

Abe's BBQ
616 State Street
Clarksdale
www.abesbbq.com
(662) 624-9947

Doe's Eat Place
502 Nelson Street
Greenville
www.doeseatplace.com
(662) 334-3315

LEATHA'S BAR-B-QUE INN
6374 U.S. 98
Hattiesburg (601) 271-6003

The Pig Out Inn Barbeque
116 South Canal Street
Natchez (601) 442-8050

THE SHED BARBEQUE & BLUES JOINT
7501 State 57
Ocean Springs
www.theshedbbq.com
(228) 875-9590

GOLDIE'S TRAIL BAR-B-Q
2430 South Frontage Road
Vicksburg (601) 636-9839

Smoked Strip Steaks

Strip steaks offer a lot of surface area relative to their total size, which allows them to absorb a maximum amount of smoke. Serve thin slices of the steak over rice pilaf.

Prep: 15 min.; **Soak:** 30 min.; **Chill:** 30 min.; **Cook:** 3 min.; **Grill:** 1 hr., 15 min.; **Stand:** 5 min.

2 cups wood chips

2 tsp. freshly ground black pepper

1 tsp. garlic powder

½ tsp. salt

¼ tsp. dry mustard

2 (12-oz.) New York strip or sirloin strip steaks, trimmed

2 tsp. Worcestershire sauce

1. Soak wood chips in water 30 minutes; drain.
2. Combine pepper, garlic powder, salt, and mustard, and rub evenly over both sides of steaks. Place coated steaks in a large zip-top plastic bag; add Worcestershire sauce. Seal and shake to coat. Marinate in refrigerator 30 minutes.
3. Prepare grill for indirect grilling, heating one side to low and leaving one side with no heat. Maintain temperature at 250° to 300°.
4. Heat a large, heavy skillet over high heat. Remove steaks from bag, and discard marinade. Coat pan with cooking spray. Add steaks to pan; cook 1½ minutes on each side or until browned. Remove from pan.
5. Place wood chips on hot coals. Place a disposable aluminum foil pan on unheated side of grill. Pour 2 cups water in pan. Coat the grill rack with cooking spray, and place on grill. Place steaks on grill rack over foil pan on unheated side. Close lid; cook 1 hour and 15 minutes or until a thermometer inserted into steak registers 145° (medium-rare) or until desired degree of doneness. Remove steaks from grill; cover and let stand 5 minutes. Cut steaks across grain into thin slices. **Makes** 6 servings.

'Que and A

Q: My wholesale club sells bulk packages of steaks for cheap. Is it okay for me to freeze them, and, if so, what's the best way to keep them from getting freezer burn?

A: Meats are best when fresh, but it's nice to be able to keep some on hand in the freezer. The key is to keep air off the surface of the meat. The best way to prevent freezer burn is to wrap each steak in plastic wrap and seal as tightly as possible. Place them in a large zip-top freezer bag, and place in a freezer that is as cold as possible. Or, if you have a vacuum sealer, use it to greatly prolong freshness by removing all the air surrounding the meat. Be sure to date and label your bag—steaks should keep for about three months.

Smoked Flank Steak

Hickory wood chips impart a savory note, though you can experiment with other types of wood. Marinating the steak overnight allows for the most robust flavor. But if you're pressed for time, simply rub the spice blend over the steak and grill it.

Prep: 30 min.; **Chill:** 8 hr.; **Soak:** 1 hr.; **Grill:** 1 hr., 5 min.; **Stand:** 5 min.

2 tsp. ground cumin

2 tsp. Spanish smoked paprika

½ tsp. kosher salt

½ tsp. ground coriander

⅛ tsp. ground red pepper

4 garlic cloves, minced

1 (1½-lb.) flank steak, trimmed

2 cups hickory wood chips

1. Combine first 6 ingredients in a small bowl, stirring well. Place steak in a shallow dish; rub spice mixture evenly over both sides of steak. Cover and refrigerate 8 hours or overnight.

2. Soak wood chips in water 1 hour; drain.

3. Prepare grill for indirect grilling, heating one side to low and leaving one side with no heat. Maintain temperature at 250° to 300°.

4. Place wood chips on hot coals. Place a disposable aluminum foil pan on unheated side of grill. Pour 2 cups water in pan. Coat grill rack with cooking spray; place on grill. Place steak on grill rack over foil pan on unheated side. Close lid; grill 1 hour and 5 minutes or until steak is medium-rare or until desired degree of doneness, turning once. Remove steak from grill; cover and let stand 5 minutes. Cut steak diagonally across grain into thin slices. **Makes** 6 servings.

tools of the trade

Tongs: Tongs are a versatile tool and are great for flipping most foods, from steaks to grilled vegetables. They grip food easily without piercing—a culprit for dryness—and they keep you at a safe distance from hot coals. Look for tongs with long handles and a spring hinge.

Championship Pork Butt

World championship barbecue guru Chris Lilly shares his recipe for prize-winning pork butt.

Prep: 20 min.; **Grill:** 7 hr.; **Stand:** 15 min.

1 (6- to 8-lb.) bone-in pork shoulder roast (Boston butt)

Pork Butt Injection Marinade

Pork Butt Dry Rub

1. Rinse pork roast, and pat dry. Inject top of roast at 1-inch intervals with Pork Butt Injection Marinade.
2. Coat roast with Pork Butt Dry Rub, pressing gently to adhere rub to pork.
3. Light one side of grill, heating to 250° (low) heat; leave other side unlit. Place roast over unlit side; grill, covered, 7 to 9 hours or until a meat thermometer inserted into thickest portion registers 190°, maintaining temperature inside grill between 225° and 250°. Let stand 15 minutes. Slice, shred, or chop roast. **Makes** 10 to 12 servings.

Pork Butt Injection Marinade

Prep: 5 min.

⅓ cup apple juice

⅓ cup white grape juice

¼ cup sugar

1½ Tbsp. salt

1. Stir together all ingredients in a medium bowl. Store in an airtight container in refrigerator up to 2 weeks. **Makes** about ⅔ cup.

Pork Butt Dry Rub

Prep: 10 min.

4 tsp. seasoned salt

2 tsp. dark brown sugar

1½ tsp. granulated sugar

1½ tsp. paprika

¼ tsp. garlic powder

¼ tsp. pepper

⅛ tsp. dry mustard

⅛ tsp. ground cumin

Pinch of ground ginger

1. Stir together all ingredients. Store in an airtight container up to 1 month. **Makes** about 3½ Tbsp.

Dan the Man's Pork Loin Roast

We adapted this recipe from _The Family Style Soul Food Diabetes Cookbook_ (The American Diabetes Association, 2006). It cooks over indirect heat to develop smoky flavor, and the sauce uses a sweetener made by Splenda for those who enjoy tangy-sweet sauces but try to stay away from sugar.

Prep: 15 min.; **Chill:** 2 hr.; **Grill:** 1 hr, 30. min.; **Stand:** 10 min.

½ cup lite soy sauce

1 Tbsp. Caribbean jerk seasoning

1 (3-lb.) boneless pork loin roast, trimmed

¼ cup brown sugar blend sweetener

¼ cup bourbon

Shopping tip: We tested with Splenda Brown Sugar Blend Sweetener.

1. Stir together lite soy sauce and jerk seasoning. Place roast in a 2-gal. zip-top plastic freezer bag. Pour soy sauce mixture over roast. Seal bag, and chill 2 hours, turning occasionally.

2. Preheat one side of grill, heating to medium-high heat (350° to 400°); leave other side unlit. Remove roast from marinade, discarding marinade.

3. Stir together brown sugar blend sweetener and bourbon in a microwave-safe glass measuring cup. Microwave at HIGH 1 minute or until sugar blend is dissolved, stirring after 30 seconds.

4. Place roast over lit side of grill; grill, covered, 5 minutes on each side. Baste with brown sugar blend mixture; turn and baste other side. Move pork to unlit side; grill, covered, 1 hour and 20 minutes or until a meat thermometer inserted into thickest portion registers 150°, basting after 15 minutes and 30 minutes. Remove from heat; let stand 10 minutes before slicing. **Makes** 8 servings.

Bacon-Wrapped Pork Medallions With Tomato-Corn Salsa

Prep: 20 min.; **Chill:** 2 hr.; **Grill:** 40 min.; **Stand:** 10 min.

3 (¾-lb.) pork tenderloins

2 Tbsp. olive oil

1 Tbsp. white balsamic vinegar

1½ tsp. ancho chile powder

1 tsp. coarsely ground black pepper

8 thick-cut bacon slices

Tomato-Corn Salsa

1. Cut pork into 8 (3-inch-thick) slices. Place meat, cut sides up, between 2 sheets of heavy-duty plastic wrap, and flatten to 2-inch thickness, using a rolling pin or flat side of a meat mallet.

2. Whisk together olive oil and next 3 ingredients. Rub mixture evenly over pork; cover and chill 2 hours.

3. Microwave bacon at HIGH 2 minutes or until bacon is partially cooked. Wrap sides of each pork slice with 1 bacon slice, and secure with a wooden pick.

4. Light 1 side of grill, heating to 350° to 400° (medium-high) heat; leave other side unlit. Arrange pork over lit side; grill, covered with grill lid, 5 minutes on each side. Move pork to unlit side; grill, covered, 30 to 35 minutes or until a meat thermometer registers 155°. Let stand 10 minutes. Serve with Tomato-Corn Salsa. **Makes** 8 servings.

Tomato-Corn Salsa

White balsamic vinegar has a milder flavor and won't darken the corn's color.

Prep: 15 min.; **Grill:** 8 min.; **Stand:** 10 min.

4 ears fresh corn, husks removed

2 tsp. olive oil

1 pt. grape tomatoes, halved

3 green onions, sliced

¼ cup chopped fresh basil

2 Tbsp. white balsamic vinegar

1 tsp. salt

½ tsp. pepper

1. Preheat grill to 350° to 400° (medium-high) heat. Brush corn evenly with oil. Grill, covered with grill lid, 8 minutes, turning every 2 minutes or until done. Let stand 10 minutes. Cut kernels from cobs; discard cobs.
2. Combine corn, tomatoes, and next 5 ingredients, tossing to coat. **Makes** 2 cups.

Weeknight Menu

Serves 8 hungry folks

BACON-WRAPPED PORK MEDALLIONS

Tomato Corn Salsa

GARLIC MASHED POTATOES, PAGE 249

Steamed broccoli

Lemony Ice-Cream Pie, page 275

Grilled Pork Roast With Fruit Compote

Prep: 15 min.; **Grill:** 1 hr., 1 min.; **Stand:** 10 min.

1 (4-lb.) boneless pork loin roast, trimmed

Kitchen string

2 tsp. salt

1 tsp. pepper

2 Tbsp. chopped garlic

1 Tbsp. finely chopped fresh rosemary

1 Tbsp. chopped fresh thyme

2 Tbsp. olive oil

Fruit Compote

1. Tie pork with kitchen string, securing at 2-inch intervals. Sprinkle pork with salt and pepper. Stir together garlic and next 3 ingredients. Rub over pork.

2. Light 1 side of grill, heating to 350° to 400° (medium-high) heat; leave other side unlit. Place pork over lit side, and grill, covered with grill lid, 8 to 10 minutes on each side or until browned. Move pork over unlit side, and grill, covered, 45 minutes or until a meat thermometer inserted into thickest portion registers 150°. Let stand 10 minutes before slicing. Serve with Fruit Compote. **Makes** 10 servings.

Time-saving tip: If you'd rather not mess with tying the roast, ask the butcher to do it for you.

Fruit Compote

Prep: 15 min.; **Cook:** 25 min.

16 dried Mission figlets, quartered

1 Granny Smith apple, diced

12 dried apricots, thinly sliced

½ cup seedless red grapes, halved

½ cup chopped red onion

½ cup dry white wine

½ cup cider vinegar

1 cup sugar

½ tsp. salt

½ tsp. pepper

1. Combine all ingredients in a 3-qt. saucepan, and cook over medium heat, stirring occasionally, 25 minutes or until thickened and liquid is reduced by three-fourths. (Mixture will continue to thicken as it cools.) Serve warm or at room temperature. **Makes** 2 cups.

Ingredient tip: We tested with Blue Ribbon Orchard Choice Mission Figlets. Twelve dried Mission figs, coarsely chopped, may be substituted.

Grilled Pork Loin Roast

Prep: 20 min.; **Chill:** 4 hr.; **Grill:** 1 hr., 10 min.; **Stand:** 10 min.

Soda Pop-and-Soy Marinade

1 (2½-lb.) boneless pork loin roast

1 tsp. salt

½ tsp. pepper

Kitchen string

Garnish: fresh flat-leaf parsley sprigs

1. Place Soda Pop-and-Soy Marinade in a shallow dish or large zip-top plastic freezer bag. Pierce pork loin roast several times with a knife; add roast to marinade, and turn to coat. Cover or seal, and chill 4 to 6 hours, turning occasionally.
2. Light 1 side of grill, heating to 350° to 400° (medium-high) heat; leave other side unlit.
3. Remove roast from marinade, discarding marinade. Pat roast dry; sprinkle with salt and pepper. Tie with kitchen string, securing at 2-inch intervals.
4. Place roast over lit side of grill, and grill, covered with grill lid, 5 minutes on each side or until browned. Transfer roast to unlit side, and grill, covered, 1 hour or until a meat thermometer inserted into thickest portion registers 150°. Remove from grill, and let stand 10 minutes before slicing. Garnish with parsley sprigs, if desired. **Makes** 6 to 8 servings.

Soda Pop-and-Soy Marinade

Prep: 10 min.

1 cup lemon-lime soft drink

1 Tbsp. light brown sugar

3 Tbsp. soy sauce

2 Tbsp. olive oil

1 Tbsp. Worcestershire sauce

2 garlic cloves, pressed

¾ tsp. ground ginger

⅛ tsp. ground cloves

1. Whisk together lemon-lime soft drink and remaining ingredients until thoroughly blended. Use immediately. **Makes** about 1⅓ cups.

Ingredient tip: Don't use diet soft drink—the pork won't brown, and the aftertaste will be unpleasant.

Honey-Soy Appetizer Ribs

Have the butcher cut the ribs in half crosswise to make appetizer-size ribs. This recipe simmers the ribs before grilling, a Southern trick to tenderize them without having to grill them quite as long over indirect heat.

Prep: 15 min.; **Cook:** 30 min.; **Grill:** 1 hr., 30 min.; **Stand:** 10 min.

2 slabs pork spareribs
(about 4 lb.)

1 cup honey

⅓ cup soy sauce

3 Tbsp. sherry (optional)

2 tsp. garlic powder

½ tsp. dried crushed red
pepper

Garnishes: sesame seeds,
thinly sliced green onions

Quick Asian Barbecue Sauce
(optional)

1. Rinse and pat ribs dry. Remove thin membrane from back of ribs by slicing into it with a knife and then pulling it off.
2. Bring ribs and water to cover to a boil in a large Dutch oven over medium-high heat; reduce heat to medium, and simmer 30 minutes. Drain and pat dry. Place ribs in a 13- x 9-inch baking dish.
3. Stir together honey and next 4 ingredients; pour over ribs.
4. Light 1 side of grill, heating to 350° to 400° (medium-high) heat; leave other side unlit. Arrange ribs over unlit side of grill, reserving sauce in dish. Grill, covered with grill lid, 45 minutes. Reposition rib slabs, placing slab closest to heat source away from heat and moving other slab closer to heat. Grill, covered, 45 minutes to 1 hour or until tender, repositioning ribs and basting with reserved sauce every 20 minutes. Remove ribs from grill, and let stand 10 minutes. Cut ribs, slicing between bones. Garnish, if desired. Serve with Quick Asian Barbecue Sauce, if desired. **Makes** 8 appetizer servings.

Quick Asian Barbecue Sauce

Prep: 5 min.

½ cup barbecue sauce

2 Tbsp. soy sauce

1 tsp. Asian Sriracha
hot chili sauce

1. Stir together all ingredients until blended. **Makes** ½ cup.

'Que
and A

Q: My rib recipe says to remove the thin membrane on the back of the ribs. Do I really need to do that?

A: Yes. Removing the membrane allows the smoke and seasoning to penetrate the meat.

Fall-off-the-Bone Baby Back Ribs

We adapted this recipe from Sara Foster's book *Fresh Every Day* (Clarkson Potter, 2005). Sara owns Foster's Market in Durham and Chapel Hill, North Carolina.

Prep: 10 min.; **Bake:** 3 hr.; **Grill:** 20 min.; **Stand:** 10 min.

1 large onion, sliced

2 slabs baby back ribs (about 3½ pounds)

1 (12-oz.) bottle beer

Sea salt and freshly ground pepper, to taste

2 cups Chipotle Maple Barbecue Sauce

1. Preheat oven to 350°. Spread onion slices evenly on a rimmed baking sheet, and place ribs, bone side down, on top. Pour beer over ribs, sprinkle with sea salt and pepper, and cover tightly with foil. Bake 3 hours or until tender.

2. Preheat grill to 300° to 350° (medium) heat. Brush both sides of ribs with Chipotle Maple Barbecue Sauce. Grill, meat side down, 10 to 15 minutes or until slightly charred and crispy, basting several times with sauce. Flip ribs over, and baste cooked side liberally. Grill, covered, 10 to 15 minutes more, basting often. Remove from heat; let stand 10 minutes. Cut individual ribs apart, and serve warm. **Makes** 4 to 6 servings.

Chipotle Maple Barbecue Sauce

Prep: 15 min.; **Cook:** 30 min.

1 (28-oz.) can crushed tomatoes

½ cup maple syrup

½ cup firmly packed light brown sugar

3 canned chipotle peppers in adobo sauce, diced

1 cup white vinegar

¼ cup Worcestershire sauce

½ cup apple cider

Juice of 2 lemons

4 garlic cloves, minced

2 Tbsp. dry mustard

2 tsp. sea salt

2 tsp. freshly ground pepper

1. Combine all ingredients in a heavy saucepan. Bring to a boil over medium-high heat. Reduce heat, and simmer 30 to 35 minutes or until sauce is thickened and reduced by one-fourth. Refrigerate in an airtight container up to 2 weeks. **Makes** about 4½ cups.

Make-ahead tip: Prepare this sauce up to two weeks ahead. Besides the rib recipe, the sauce is great for chicken, roasted pork, and burgers.

tips from the **pit master**

Apply sauces towards the end of your cook time. The sugars in most barbecue sauces will burn if applied too early and cooked too long.

Arkansas

Here's where to get great 'Q in the state.

JJ's Barbeque & Catfish

1000 East Main Street
El Dorado
(870) 862-1777
www.jjsbbq.com

McClard's Bar-B-Q

505 Albert Pike
Hot Springs
(501) 623-9665
www.mcclards.com

Sim's Bar-B-Que

2415 Broadway Street
Little Rock
(501) 372-6868

Troy's Baby Back Ribs

Prep: 20 min.; **Chill:** 8 hrs.; **Grill:** 6 hrs., 20 min.; **Stand:** 10 min.

3 slabs baby back pork ribs

Barbecue Rub

Hickory wood chips

Apple juice

Barbecue sauce

1. Remove thin membrane from back of ribs by slicing into it with a knife and then pulling. Sprinkle meat generously with Barbecue Rub. Massage rub into meat. Wrap tightly with plastic wrap, and chill 8 hours.

2. Prepare a hot fire by piling charcoal on 1 side of grill, leaving other side empty. (For gas grills, light only 1 side.) Place cooking grate on grill. Arrange ribs over unlit side.

3. Grill 2 hours, covered with grill lid, adding 5 to 7 charcoal pieces every 45 minutes to 1 hour, and keeping temperature between 225° and 250°. Add a handful of hickory chips to the charcoal every 20 to 30 minutes. Spritz ribs with apple juice from a squeeze-trigger sprayer each time you add wood chips and coals.

4. Reposition slabs occasionally, placing the one closest to the heat source in the back and adding hickory chips and coals as needed. Grill 2 more hours. Remove ribs from grill, and place on heavy-duty aluminum foil. Spritz with apple juice; tightly seal. Place foil-wrapped ribs back on the grill; cook 2 more hours. Remove ribs from foil, place flat on grill, and baste generously with your favorite barbecue sauce. Grill 20 more minutes. Remove from grill, and let stand 10 minutes. **Makes** 6 servings.

Barbecue Rub

Prep: 10 min.

1 cup firmly packed dark brown sugar

½ cup granulated garlic

½ cup kosher salt

½ cup paprika

2 Tbsp. granulated onion

1 Tbsp. dry mustard

1 Tbsp. Creole seasoning

1 Tbsp. chili powder

1 Tbsp. ground red pepper

1 Tbsp. ground cumin

1 Tbsp. ground black pepper

1. Stir together all ingredients in a bowl. Store in an airtight container. **Makes** about 3 cups.

tips from the **pit master**

For ribs that will be "fall-off-the-bone tender," cook them until they bend to the ground when picked up by tongs.

Carefully remove the thin membrane on the back of ribs.

Sprinkle meat with Barbecue Rub.

61

Sweet-Hot Baby Back Ribs

Our directions are for a two-burner gas grill. If you have a three-burner grill, light both sides, and leave the center burner off.

Prep: 30 min.; **Chill:** 8 hr.; **Stand:** 40 min.; **Grill:** 2 hr., 30 min.

2 Tbsp. ground ginger

1 tsp. salt

1 tsp. black pepper

½ tsp. dried crushed red pepper

3 slabs baby back ribs (about 2 lb. each)

2 limes, halved

Sweet-Hot 'Cue Sauce

1. Combine first 4 ingredients in a small bowl.

2. Rinse and pat ribs dry. If desired, remove thin membrane from back of ribs by slicing into it with a knife and then pulling it off. (This will make ribs more tender.)

3. Rub ribs with cut sides of limes, squeezing as you rub. Massage ginger mixture into meat, covering all sides. Wrap ribs tightly with plastic wrap, and place in zip-top plastic freezer bags or a 13- x 9-inch baking dish; seal or cover, and chill 8 hours. Let ribs stand at room temperature 30 minutes before grilling. Remove plastic wrap.

4. Light 1 side of grill, heating to medium-high heat (350° to 400°); leave other side unlit. Place rib slabs over unlit side, stacking 1 on top of the other.

5. Grill, covered with grill lid, 40 minutes. Reposition rib slabs, moving bottom slab to the top, and grill 40 minutes. Reposition 1 more time, moving bottom slab to the top; grill 40 minutes.

6. Lower grill temperature to medium heat (300° to 350°); unstack rib slabs, and place side by side over unlit side of grill. Cook ribs 30 more minutes, basting with half of Sweet-Hot 'Cue Sauce. Remove ribs from grill, and let stand 10 minutes. Cut ribs, slicing between bones. Serve ribs with remaining Sweet-Hot 'Cue Sauce. **Makes** 6 servings.

Sweet-Hot 'Cue Sauce

Prep: 10 min.; **Cook:** 30 min.

2 (10-oz.) bottles sweet chili sauce

2 cups ketchup

⅓ cup firmly packed dark brown sugar

1 tsp. ground ginger

1 tsp. pepper

½ tsp. dried crushed red pepper

Shopping tip: We tested with Maggi Taste of Asia Sweet Chili Sauce.

1. Combine all ingredients in a saucepan over medium-high heat. Bring mixture to a boil; reduce heat, and simmer 30 minutes. **Makes** 4 cups.

tips for a tailgate Frightful of flare-ups? Be prepared to tame any flames by traveling to the game with a small spray bottle of water to squirt the coals if things get a little out of hand. Trimming any excess fat off the meat will also help to prevent flare-ups and charring.

Apricot-Pineapple Sweet Ribs

The flavorful seasoning used to baste these ribs from pitmaster Chris Lilly takes the South's favorite finger foods to new heights.

Prep: 20 min.; **Grill:** 3 hr., 30 min.

2 slabs baby back ribs (about 2 lb. each)

Rib Dry Rub

Rib Liquid Seasoning

Sweet Barbecue Glaze

1. Remove thin membrane from back of each slab by slicing into it and then pulling it off. (This will make ribs more tender.) Generously apply Rib Dry Rub on both sides of ribs, pressing gently to adhere.

2. Light 1 side of grill, heating to 250° (low) heat; leave other side unlit. Place slabs, meat sides up, over unlit side; grill, covered, 2 hours and 15 minutes, maintaining temperature between 225° and 250°.

3. Remove slabs from grill. Place each slab, meat side down, on a large piece of heavy-duty aluminum foil. (Foil should be large enough to completely wrap slab.) Pour ½ cup of Rib Liquid Seasoning over each slab. Tightly wrap each slab in foil. Return slabs to unlit side of grill. Grill, covered, 1 hour. Remove slabs; unwrap and discard foil. Brush Sweet Barbecue Glaze on both sides of slabs. Grill slabs, covered, on unlit side of grill 15 minutes or until caramelized. **Makes** 4 to 6 servings.

Rib Dry Rub

Prep: 5 min.

¼ cup firmly packed dark brown sugar

4 tsp. garlic salt

4 tsp. chili powder

2 tsp. salt

1 tsp. ground black pepper

½ tsp. celery salt

¼ tsp. ground white pepper

¼ tsp. ground red pepper

¼ tsp. ground cinnamon

1. Stir together all ingredients. Store in an airtight container up to 1 month. **Makes** about ½ cup.

Rib Liquid Seasoning

Prep: 5 min.

½ cup pineapple juice

½ cup apricot nectar

1 Tbsp. Rib Dry Rub

1½ tsp. balsamic vinegar

1½ tsp. minced garlic

1. Stir together all ingredients. Store in an airtight container in refrigerator up to 2 weeks. **Makes** about 1 cup.

Sweet Barbecue Glaze

Prep: 5 min.

1¼ cups premium tomato-based barbecue sauce

¼ cup honey

Shopping tip: We tested with Big Bob Gibson Bar-B-Q Championship Red Sauce.

1. Stir together all ingredients. Store in an airtight container in refrigerator up to 2 weeks. **Makes** about 1½ cups.

Baby Back Ribs With Jackie's Dry Rub

These ribs from the McCalla family who own Jackie M's Catering in Augusta, Georgia, are cooked without any sauce.

Prep: 20 min.; Soak: 30 min.; **Grill:** 3 hr.

Mesquite wood chips

2 slabs baby back ribs (about 4 lb.)

2 Tbsp. mesquite liquid smoke

2 Tbsp. olive oil

3 Tbsp. Jackie's Dry Rub

1. Soak wood chips in water 30 minutes. Prepare smoker according to manufacturer's directions, bringing internal temperature to 225° to 250°; maintain temperature for 15 to 20 minutes.

2. Rinse and pat ribs dry. If desired, remove thin membrane from back of ribs by slicing into it with a knife and pulling it off. Coat both sides of ribs with liquid smoke and olive oil. Sprinkle ribs with Jackie's Dry Rub, and rub into ribs.

3. Drain mesquite wood chips, and place on coals. Place pork ribs on lower cooking grate; cover with smoker lid.

4. Smoke ribs, maintaining temperature inside smoker between 225° and 250°, for 3 to 4 hours or until tender. **Makes** 4 to 6 servings.

Jackie's Dry Rub

When grinding the spices it is best to use a mortar and pestle or a small spice grinder. The rub produced by a food processor is too coarse.

Prep: 5 min.

---

2 Tbsp. dried rosemary

2 Tbsp. dried thyme

2 Tbsp. kosher salt

2 Tbsp. white peppercorns

1. Combine all ingredients in a mortar bowl or spice grinder; grind using a pestle or grinder until herbs and pepper become a medium-fine powder. Store in an airtight container in a cool, dark place up to 6 months. **Makes** about ½ cup.

tips from the pit master

Clean dirty grill grates with a spray bottle of water and crumbled aluminum foil held by a pair of tongs. Spraying the water on hot grates will "deglaze" them and make cleaning easier.

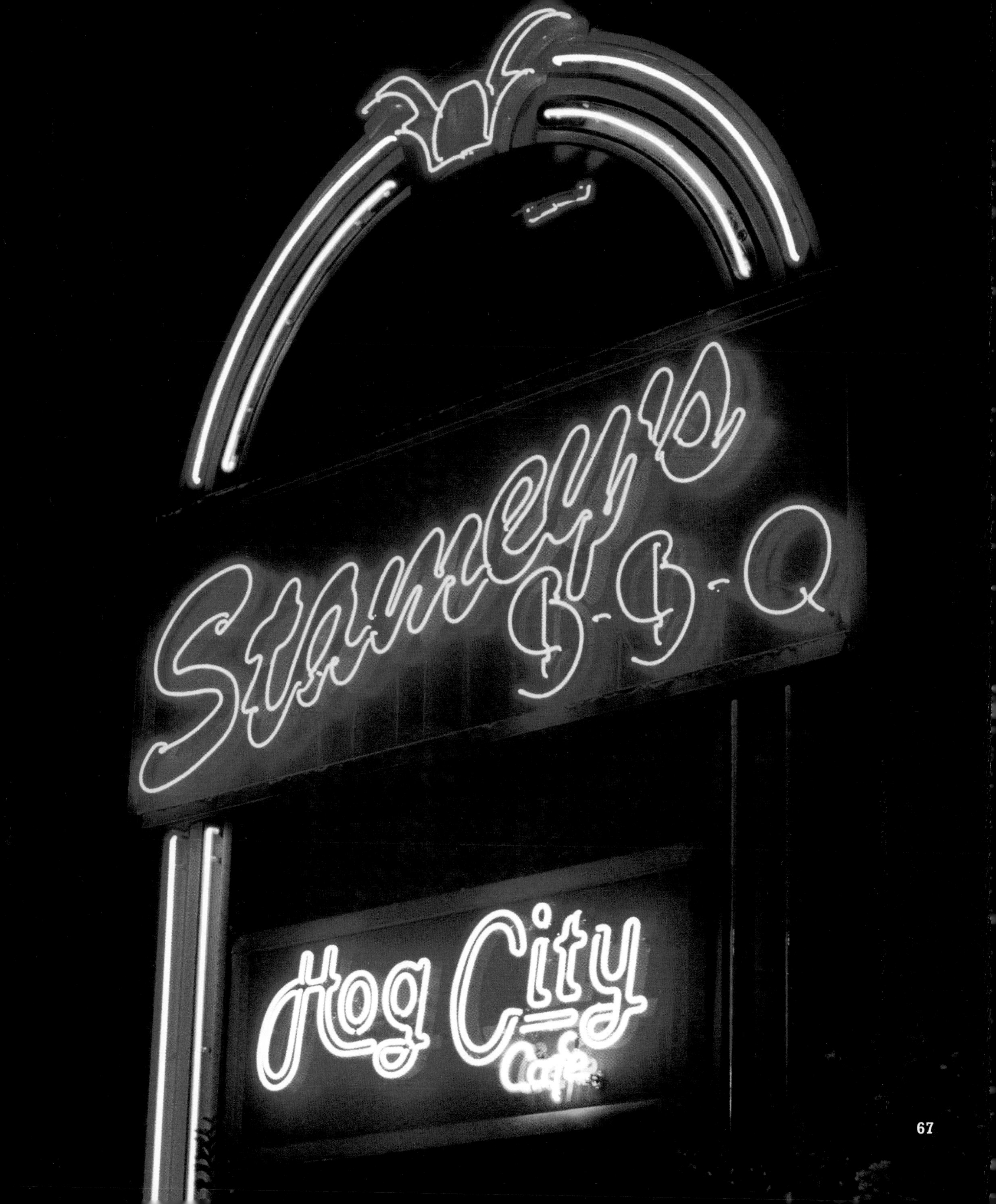
Stamey's
B-B-Q
Hog City
Cafe

Pork Ribs from Crook's Corner

Grilled ribs are one of the specialties at Crook's Corner Cafe & Bar in Chapel Hill, North Carolina, which has been called "sacred ground for Southern foodies" by *The New York Times*. Chef Bill Smith's signature sauce is made with blackstrap molasses and hot sauce.

Prep: 10 min.; **Bake:** 3 hr.; **Stand:** 20 min.; **Grill:** 10 min.

2 racks St. Louis-style ribs (2 ½ lb.)

½ cup olive oil

Sea salt, to taste

Freshly ground pepper, to taste

Bill's Blackstrap Barbecue Sauce

Shopping tip: St. Louis-style ribs are spareribs with the top boney and fatty section trimmed off, leaving single vertical bones. They are easier to eat and somewhat leaner than regular spareribs.

1. Preheat oven to 350°. Drizzle both sides of ribs with oil; sprinkle with sea salt and pepper. Place on a baking rack over rimmed baking sheet. Add 1½ cups water to baking sheet, and cover tightly with foil. Roast 3 hours or until ribs are tender. (Meat should separate easily from bone.)
2. Remove ribs from oven, and let stand at least 20 minutes.
3. Preheat grill to 300° to 350° (medium) heat. Brush ribs on both sides with Bill's Blackstrap Barbecue Sauce, and grill, covered with grill lid, 5 to 6 minutes on each side or until heated through and slightly charred.
Makes 4 servings.

Bill's Blackstrap Barbecue Sauce

Prep: 5 min.; **Cook:** 1 hr.

2 cups firmly packed brown sugar

1 cup hot sauce

2 cups cider vinegar

½ cup blackstrap molasses

1. Combine all ingredients in a heavy nonstick saucepan, and bring to a boil. Reduce heat to low, and simmer about 1 hour or until sauce is thick and shiny. Refrigerate in an airtight container up to several weeks. **Makes** 3 cups.

Ingredient tip: Blackstrap molasses, produced from the final pressing of sugarcane, is much darker in color and higher in mineral content than regular molasses. Its complex taste, which is not purely sweet, makes for a more interesting sauce, but you can substitute the same amount of regular molasses in a pinch.

Barbecued Country-Style Ribs

Prep: 30 min.; **Cook:** 1 hr., 10 min.; **Grill:** 1 hr.

1 small onion, finely chopped

1 cup finely chopped celery

1½ Tbsp. bacon drippings

1 (15-oz.) can tomato sauce

¾ cup honey

½ cup water

¼ cup dry red wine

2 Tbsp. lemon juice

2 Tbsp. Worcestershire sauce

1 tsp. salt

½ tsp. pepper

¼ tsp. garlic powder

2 Tbsp. white vinegar

4 lb. boneless country-style ribs, cut apart

1. Preheat grill to 300° to 350° (medium) heat.

2. Sauté onion and celery in hot bacon drippings in a saucepan over medium-high heat until tender. Add tomato sauce and next 8 ingredients. Bring to a boil. Reduce heat; simmer, stirring occasionally, 1 hour. Remove from heat.

3. Combine 1 cup water and vinegar in a spray bottle.

4. Grill ribs, covered with grill lid, 1 to 1½ hours, spraying with vinegar solution and turning ribs occasionally, and basting with 1 cup sauce mixture every 30 minutes. Serve with remaining sauce mixture. **Makes** 8 servings.

Shopping tip: 4 lb. bone-in country-style pork ribs may be substituted.

Hickory-Smoked Bourbon Turkey

Prep: 30 min.; **Chill:** 2 days; **Soak:** 30 min.; **Grill:** 5 hr., 30 min.; **Stand:** 15 min.

1 (11-lb.) whole turkey, thawed

2 cups maple syrup

1 cup bourbon

1 Tbsp. pickling spice

Hickory wood chunks

1 large carrot, peeled

1 celery rib

1 medium onion, peeled and halved

1 lemon

1 Tbsp. salt

2 tsp. pepper

Garnishes: mixed greens, lemon wedges

1. Remove giblets and neck from turkey; reserve for other uses, if desired. Rinse turkey thoroughly with cold water, and pat dry.

2. Add water to a large stockpot, filling half full; stir in maple syrup, bourbon, and pickling spice. Add turkey and, if needed, additional water to cover. Cover and chill turkey 2 days.

3. Soak hickory wood chunks in water at least 30 minutes. Prepare charcoal fire in smoker; let fire burn 20 to 30 minutes.

4. Remove turkey from water, discarding water mixture; pat dry. Cut carrot and celery in half crosswise. Stuff cavity with carrot, celery, and onion. Pierce lemon with a fork; place in neck cavity.

5. Combine salt and pepper; rub mixture over turkey. Fold wings under, and tie legs together with string, if desired.

6. Drain wood chunks, and place on coals. Place water pan in smoker, and add water to depth of fill line. Place turkey in center of lower food rack; cover with smoker lid.

7. Cook 5½ hours or until a meat thermometer inserted into thickest portion of turkey thigh registers 170°, adding additional water, charcoal, and wood chunks as needed. Remove from smoker, and let stand 15 minutes before slicing. Garnish, if desired. **Makes** 12 to 14 servings.

Mesquite-Smoked Cornish Hens

Prep: 40 min.; **Chill:** 4 hr.; **Soak:** 30 min.; **Grill:** 2 hr.

3 (1½-lb.) Cornish hens

3 small Rome apples, cored and quartered (about ¾ lb.)

1 cup fresh thyme leaves

2 Tbsp. chopped fresh parsley

½ tsp. freshly ground pepper

¼ tsp. salt

1 cup unsweetened apple juice

¼ cup soy sauce

Mesquite wood chips

Garnishes: fresh cilantro sprigs, apple slices

1. Remove giblets and neck from hens, and discard. Rinse hens with cold water; pat dry with paper towels. Stuff hens with apple quarters.

2. Loosen skin from hen breasts without totally detaching skin. Combine thyme and next 3 ingredients. Rub half of herb mixture evenly under and over skin. Tie ends of legs together with string; close body cavities, and secure with wooden picks.

3. Place hens in a 13- x 9-inch baking dish. Combine apple juice, soy sauce, and remaining herb mixture; pour evenly over hens, turning to coat. Cover and chill 4 to 8 hours, turning occasionally.

4. Soak mesquite chips in water for at least 30 minutes. Set aside.

5. Prepare charcoal fire in smoker; let burn 20 minutes.

6. Meanwhile, drain hens, reserving marinade.

7. Drain mesquite chips, and place on coals. Place water pan in smoker; add reserved marinade and hot water to depth of fill line. Coat grate with cooking spray. Place hens on cold cooking grate.

8. Cook, covered, 2 hours or until a meat thermometer inserted into meaty part of thigh registers 170° or desired doneness. Garnish, if desired. **Makes** 6 servings.

Harvest Party

Serves 6 hungry folks

SAGE-SMOKED CHAMPAGNE QUAIL

Smoked Gouda Grits, page 249

Grilled Artichokes and Asparagus, page 257

CARAMEL-PECAN BARS, PAGE 265

Sage-Smoked Champagne Quail

Prep: 30 min.; **Chill:** 1 hr.; **Soak:** 30 min.; **Grill:** 2 hr.

12 quail, dressed

1 (7.5-milliliter) bottle Champagne

4 sweet yellow apples, diced

½ tsp. salt

1 (0.4-oz.) jar dried sage, divided

12 pepper-cured bacon slices

Hickory chips

4 cups apple cider

1. Combine quail and Champagne in a large bowl; cover and chill 1 hour. Drain, discarding marinade.

2. Combine apple, salt, and 1 tsp. sage; stuff quail with apple mixture, and wrap a bacon slice around each quail, securing ends with a wooden pick. Chill.

3. Soak hickory chips in water at least 30 minutes; moisten remaining sage with water.

4. Prepare charcoal fire in smoker; let burn 15 to 20 minutes.

5. Drain chips; place chips and one-third of remaining sage on coals.

6. Place water pan in smoker; add apple cider.

7. Place quail, breast side up, on upper food rack. Cover with lid.

8. Cook 2 hours or until done, adding remaining sage at 30-minute intervals. **Makes** 6 servings.

Beer-Can Chicken

Prep: 20 min.; **Chill:** 8 hrs.; **Grill:** 1 hr., 10 min.; **Stand:** 10 min.

3 (2- to 3-lb.) whole chickens

4 (12-oz.) cans beer, divided

1 (8-oz.) bottle Italian dressing

¼ to ⅓ cup fajita seasoning

1. Place each chicken in a large zip-top freezer bag. Combine 1 can beer, Italian dressing, and fajita seasoning; pour evenly over chickens. Seal bags, and chill 8 hours, turning occasionally.

2. Remove chicken from marinade, discarding marinade. Open remaining 3 cans beer. Place each chicken upright onto a beer can, fitting into cavity. Pull legs forward to form a tripod, allowing chicken to stand upright.

3. Prepare a hot fire by piling charcoal on 1 side of grill, leaving other side empty. (For gas grills, only light 1 side.) Place food grate on grill. Place chickens upright on unlit side of grill. Grill, covered with grill lid, 1 hour and 10 minutes or until golden and a meat thermometer inserted in thigh reaches 170°. Carefully remove cans; cut chickens into quarters. **Makes** 12 servings.

tips from the **pit master**

Cooked poultry that looks a little pink is done as long as you've cooked it to the proper temperature. Always rely on a meat thermometer to determine doneness.

"Two things fundamental to great barbecue are the right temperature and smoke." Troy Black

74

Smoked Lemon-Chipotle Chickens

On a chilly day, the chicken will take longer to cook—up to 45 minutes more. Don't skip the step of tying the chicken with string; the more compact the chicken, the better the smoking results will be.

Prep: 45 min.; **Soak:** 30 min.; **Grill:** 3 hr., 30 min.; **Stand:** 10 min.

---

1 small sweet onion, quartered

8 large garlic cloves, peeled

¾ cup fresh lemon juice

¼ cup olive oil

3 Tbsp. white vinegar

3 chicken bouillon cubes

3 canned chipotle peppers in adobo sauce

2 Tbsp. adobo sauce from can

2 tsp. salt, divided

3 (4½-lb.) whole chickens

Kitchen string

2½ cups hickory or oak wood chips

1. Process sweet onion, next 7 ingredients, and ¾ tsp. salt in a food processor or blender until smooth, stopping to scrape down sides. Set mixture aside.

2. Remove excess skin from necks and cavities of chickens, if desired. Starting at large cavities, loosen skin from breasts and legs by inserting fingers and gently pushing between skin and meat. (Do not completely detach skin.)

3. Place chickens in a large roasting pan. Using a bulb baster, squeeze lemon-chipotle mixture evenly into chicken cavities and under skin on breasts and legs.

4. Sprinkle chickens evenly with remaining 1¼ tsp. salt. Tuck wings under, if desired. Position the center of a 3-foot piece of kitchen string under back of one chicken near tail. Wrap string around legs and around body of chicken. Tie securely at neck. Repeat with remaining chickens.

5. Soak wood chips in water for at least 30 minutes. Set aside.

6. Prepare smoker according to manufacturer's directions. Bring internal temperature to 225° to 250°, and maintain temperature for 15 to 20 minutes. Place chickens on upper cooking grate; cover with smoker lid.

7. Cook chickens, maintaining the temperature inside the smoker between 225° and 250°, for 1½ hours. Drain reserved wood chips, and place on coals. Cover with smoker lid; smoke chickens 2 to 2½ hours more or until a meat thermometer inserted into thighs registers 170°. Remove chickens from smoker; cover loosely with aluminum foil, and let stand 10 minutes or until thermometer registers 175° before slicing. **Makes** 12 servings.

tips from the **pit master**

This recipe also works well with chicken pieces. Allow white meat breasts to reach 165° and dark meat (thighs, wings, and drumsticks) to reach 170° to 175°.

Mr. Floyd's Barbecue Chicken

Prep: 5 min.; **Cook:** 15 min.; **Soak:** 30 min.; **Grill:** 50 min.

2 cups hickory wood chips

¼ cup butter

1 cup white wine vinegar

1 cup water

¼ cup dry mustard

4 tsp. brown sugar

4 tsp. Worcestershire sauce

4 tsp. red hot sauce

1 (3-lb.) whole chicken, cut into quarters

1. Preheat grill according to directions below. Cook first 7 ingredients in a large saucepan over low heat, stirring occasionally, 15 minutes or until mixture is heated; do not simmer.

2. Reserve 1 cup vinegar sauce to serve with chicken.

3. Dip chicken in remaining sauce, and place on grill.

4. Grill chicken according to directions below, basting every 30 minutes by dipping in sauce and returning to grill (do not dip chicken the last 5 minutes of cooking).

5. Place cooked chicken in reserved 1 cup sauce, and cover to keep warm until serving. **Makes** 2 cups sauce for 4 barbecued chicken quarters.

For Gas Grills

Indirect Cooking: Place 2 cups hickory, mesquite, or other wood chips in the center of a large square of heavy-duty aluminum foil; fold into a rectangle, and seal. Punch holes in top of packet. Preheat one side of grill, leaving center empty, for 20 minutes. Place packet on cooking grate over unlit side. Grill, covered with grill lid, 2 hours and 15 minutes or until done (170°). Baste as directed.

Direct Cooking: Preheat grill over low heat, under 300°, for 20 minutes. Place chicken, skin side up, on cooking grate. Grill, covered with grill lid, over low heat 1 hour and 15 minutes or until done (170°). (Don't turn chicken.) Baste as directed.

For Charcoal Grills

Indirect Cooking: Soak 2 cups hickory wood chips in cold water for 30 minutes; drain. (Wood chips for the gas grill are not soaked in water because they're encased in foil and placed on the cooking grate.) Prepare fire by piling charcoal on each side of grill, leaving center empty. Let charcoal burn for 30 minutes, or until flames disappear and coals turn white. Sprinkle chips over hot coals. Arrange chicken, skin side up, on cooking grate in center of grill (not directly over coals). Cook covered with grill lid, for 50 minutes to 1 hour or until done (170°). (Don't turn chicken.) Baste as directed.

Grilling tip: For these methods, we prefer to use a 3-lb. whole chicken cut into quarters, which tend to cook more evenly. If using chicken pieces, remove drumsticks and wings from the grill a little earlier to keep them from burning.

Smoked King Crab Legs and Lobster Tails

Prep: 20 min.; **Soak:** 30 min.; **Grill:** 20 min. (crab legs), 45 min. (lobster tails)

Apple or alder wood chunks

1 cup butter, melted

¼ cup fresh lemon juice

1 Tbsp. minced fresh parsley

½ tsp. lemon zest

Pinch of salt

5 lb. frozen king crab legs, thawed

4 frozen lobster tails, thawed (about 2 lb.)

1. Soak wood chunks in water to cover at least 30 minutes.

2. Prepare charcoal fire in smoker; let burn 15 to 20 minutes. Drain chunks, and place on coals. Place water pan in smoker; add water to fill line.

3. Stir together butter and next 4 ingredients. Divide lemon-butter mixture in half. Crack crab legs, and split lobster tails. Brush lobster and crab with half of mixture; set aside remaining mixture.

4. Coat cooking grate with cooking spray; place in smoker. Arrange crab legs and lobster tails on grate; cover with grill lid. Smoke crab about 20 minutes and lobster 45 minutes to 1 hour or until flesh is white and firm.

5. Serve with reserved lemon-butter mixture. **Makes** 4 servings.

Hickory-Smoked Barbecue Shrimp

For easier cleanup, cover the dish inside and out with aluminum foil.

Prep: 20 min.; **Soak:** 30 min.; **Grill:** 15 min.

2 cups hickory chips

3 lb. unpeeled, large raw shrimp

3 lemons, sliced

½ to ⅔ cup hickory-flavored barbecue sauce

½ cup dry shrimp-and-crab boil seasoning

1 tsp. pepper

1 tsp. hot sauce

¾ cup butter, cut up

¾ cup dry white wine

1. Soak wood chips in water at least 30 minutes.
2. Prepare charcoal fire in grill; let burn 15 to 20 minutes.
3. Drain chips, and place on coals.
4. Place layers of shrimp and lemon slices alternately in dish; brush with barbecue sauce. Sprinkle with shrimp-and-crab boil seasoning, pepper, and hot sauce; dot with butter. Add wine to dish.
5. Place dish on grill rack, and cook, covered with grill lid, 15 to 20 minutes or just until shrimp turn pink, stirring once. **Makes** 8 servings.

Shopping tip: We tested with Kraft Thick 'n Spicy Hickory Smoked Barbecue Sauce and McCormick Shrimp-and-Crab Boil Seasoning.

Beachy Bash

HICKORY-SMOKED BARBECUE SHRIMP

Serves 3 to 4 hungry folks

Grilled Camp Corn, page 258

Boiled and buttered red potatoes

WATERMELON DAIQUIRI, PAGE 212 (DOUBLE RECIPE)

Spicy Smoked Shrimp With Orange and Lime

The deep, smoky taste from the grill complements the spicy dry rub in this easy appetizer or entrée.

Prep: 20 min.; **Soak:** 30 min.; **Chill:** 20 min.; **Grill:** 30 min.

2 cups wood chips

½ tsp. salt

½ tsp. ground red pepper

¼ tsp. freshly ground black pepper

⅛ tsp. garlic powder

⅛ tsp. ground coriander

1½ lb. **large** raw shrimp, peeled and deveined

Orange wedges

Lime wedges

1. Soak wood chips in water 30 minutes; drain.

2. Combine salt, red pepper, black pepper, garlic powder, and coriander in a small bowl. Rub mixture over shrimp. Cover and chill 20 minutes.

3. Prepare the grill for indirect grilling, heating 1 side to low and leaving 1 side with no heat. Maintain temperature at 200° to 225°.

4. Place wood chips on hot coals. Place a disposable aluminum foil pan on unheated side of grill. Pour 2 cups water in pan. Coat grill rack with cooking spray; place on grill.

5. Place shrimp on grill rack over foil pan on unheated side. Close lid; cook 30 minutes or until shrimp are done. Serve with orange and lime wedges. **Makes** 6 appetizer servings or 3 to 4 entrée servings.

Grilling tip: Shrimp are done when opaque and slightly firm.

Hot-Smoked Salmon

As chef and owner of Winterlake Lodge in Alaska, Kristen Dixon knows salmon. Although commercially smoked salmon is readily available, Kristen likes to smoke her own using alder wood and this recipe she created. Commercially smoke salmon is available either as hot smoked (kippered) or cold smoked (lox). Kristen uses hot-smoked salmon in the winter for pizzas and other savory dishes. Lox is more delicate and doesn't hold up to cooking. It's best with breakfast toast and cold appetizers.

Prep: 20 min.; **Chill:** 12 hr.; **Soak:** 30 min.; **Grill:** 15 min.

¼ cup granulated sugar

¼ cup firmly packed dark brown sugar

2 Tbsp. kosher salt

1 Tbsp. crushed black peppercorns

1 tsp. ground cardamom

1 (1-lb.) salmon fillet, pin bones removed

2 cups wood chips

1. Combine sugars, salt, peppercorns, and cardamom in a small bowl. Rub sugar mixture into salmon flesh, and pack the remaining rub around salmon. Wrap salmon tightly in plastic wrap and then in aluminum foil. Refrigerate 12 to 24 hours. Unwrap salmon, and rinse with cold water. Pat salmon dry with paper towels.
2. Soak wood chips in water 30 minutes; drain well.
3. Prepare grill for indirect grilling, heating 1 side to high and leaving 1 side with low heat.
4. Place wood chips on hot coals. Place a disposable aluminum foil pan on the unheated side of grill. Pour 2 cups water in pan. Coat food grate with cooking spray; place on grill. Place salmon on food grate over foil pan on unheated side. Close lid; cook 15 minutes or until fish flakes when tested with a fork or until desired degree of doneness. Center of fish should be opaque and warm. **Makes** 4 servings.

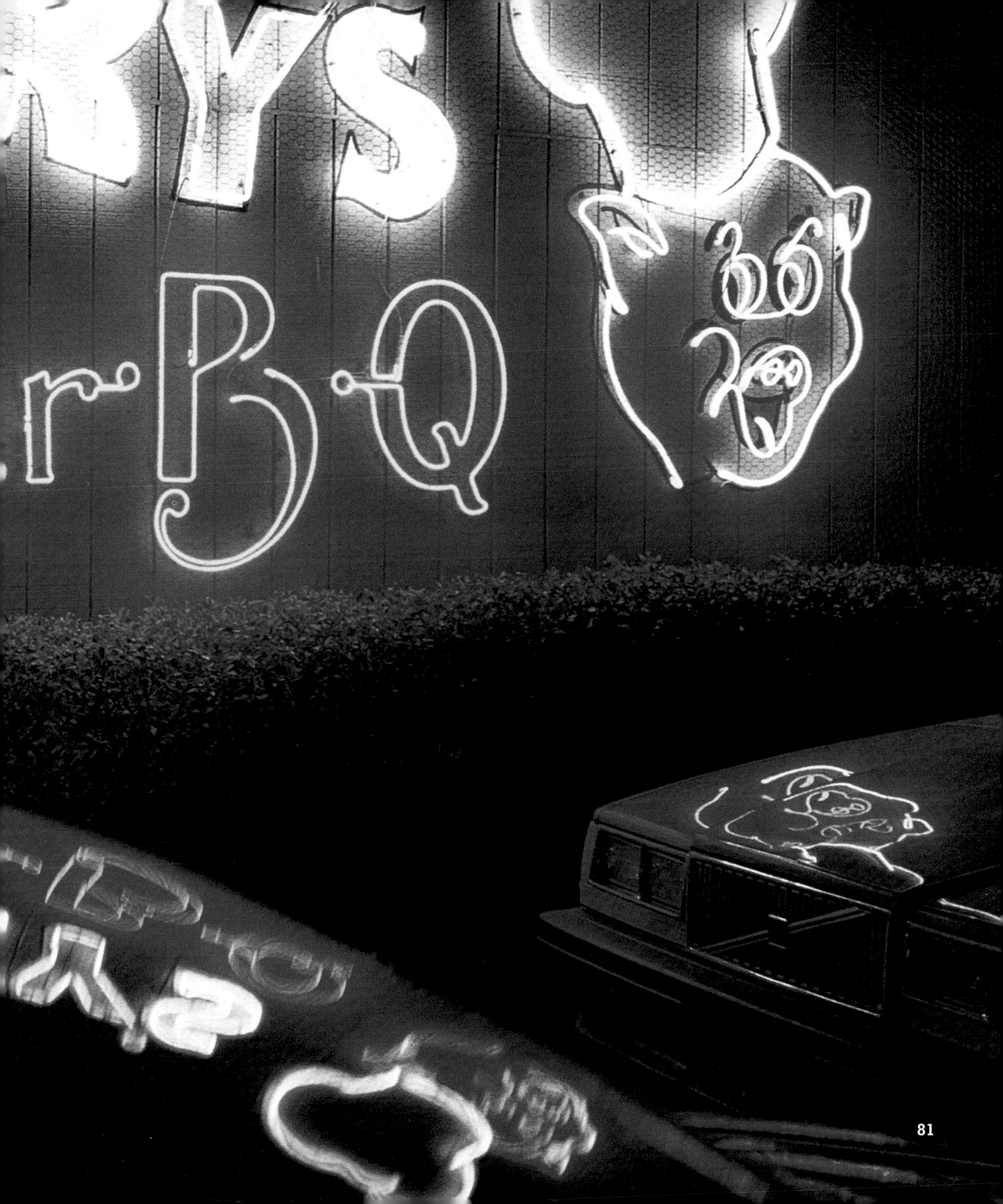

Smoked Trout

Prep: 20 min.; **Chill:** 8 hr.; **Soak:** 30 min; **Grill:** 15 min.

3 cups boiling water

1 cup firmly packed brown sugar

½ cup kosher salt

½ tsp. freshly ground black pepper

3 sprigs fresh thyme

2 (4-inch) orange rind strips

2 (8- to 10-oz.) cleaned, boned, whole trout, heads and tails removed

2 cups wood chips

Garnishes: lemon wedges, fresh thyme

1. Combine 3 cups water, sugar, salt, pepper, thyme, and rind in a large bowl; stir until sugar and salt dissolve. Combine water mixture and fish in a 13-x 9-inch baking dish. Cover and refrigerate 8 hours or overnight.

2. Soak wood chips in water 30 minutes. Drain well.

3. Prepare grill for indirect grilling, heating 1 side to medium-high and leaving 1 side with no heat. Pierce bottom of a disposable aluminum foil pan several times with the tip of a knife. Place pan on heated side of grill; add wood chips to pan.

4. Remove fish from brine; discard brine. Rinse fish with cold water; pat dry with paper towels.

5. Coat grill rack with cooking spray; place on grill. Place fish, skin side down on unheated side; cover and grill 15 minutes or until fish flakes easily when tested with a fork or until desired degree of doneness. Garnish, if desired. **Makes** 2 main-dish or 6 appetizer servings.

tools of the trade

Metal Spatula: Long-handled metal spatulas with sturdy stainless-steel blades are helpful when grilling. Look for thin, offset wide spatulas for easy flipping, and avoid pressing the meat once flipped— it'll squeeze out all the yummy juices.

Louisiana

Here's where to get great 'Q in the state.

Joe Cobb's Bossier Bar-B-Q
203 McCormick Street
Bossier City
(318) 221-6512

Grayson's Barbeque
5849 U.S. 71
Clarence
(318) 357-0166

PIG STAND RESTAURANT
318 East Main Street
Ville Platte
(337) 363-2883

Smoky Pecans

You'll eat these like popcorn, but save some for other uses. Sprinkle a few halves over green salads, or add chopped pecans to breading for catfish or pork chops.

Prep: 20 min.; **Soak:** 30 min.; **Grill:** 1 hr.

Hickory chips

2 lb. pecan halves

½ cup butter, melted

1 tsp. salt

1. Soak wood chips in water for at least 30 minutes.
2. Prepare charcoal fire in smoker; let burn 15 to 20 minutes.
3. Drain chips, and place on coals. Place water pan in smoker; add water to depth of fill line.
4. Stir together pecans, butter, and salt in a 24- x 12-inch pan. Place on upper food grate; cover with smoker lid.
5. Cook 1 hour or until golden, stirring once after 30 minutes. **Makes** 2 lb.

Grilling tip: Use a baking pan that fits your grill if the 24- x 12-inch pan is too large.

Easy Smoked Cheddar

Prep: 20 min.; **Soak:** 30 min.; **Grill:** 2 hr.; **Chill:** 24 hr.

Hickory chips

2 (16-oz.) blocks Cheddar cheese

1. Soak wood chips in water for at least 30 minutes. Prepare smoker according to manufacturer's directions, bringing internal temperature to 225°; maintain temperature for 15 to 20 minutes.

2. Place 1 cheese block on top of the other; coat with cooking spray. Place cheese lengthwise in center of a 24-inch piece of cheesecloth; tightly wrap cheesecloth around stacked cheese. Repeat procedure twice. Place wrapped cheese in a 9- x 5-inch loaf pan.

3. Drain wood chips, and place on coals. Place loaf pan on upper food grate; cover with smoker lid.

4. Smoke cheese, maintaining temperature inside smoker between 225° and 250° for 2 hours. Remove pan from smoker. Place loaf pan in refrigerator, and chill 24 hours.

5. Remove pan from refrigerator; place bottom of pan briefly in hot water to release cheese from bottom of pan. Gently unwrap cheese; cut into sticks or cubes for serving. **Makes** 2 (16-oz.) blocks.

American Royal Barbecue

Kansas City, Missouri

Even young cooks get in on the cooking competition at this annual event.

What is it?

An event for all ages that includes The World's Largest 'Cue Contest, the American Royal Livestock Show, and a Texas Hold 'Em tournament.

What is there to do?

• The younger crowd (ages 6 to 15) can participate in the Junior World Series of Barbecue contest
• Watch a horse show and rodeo at the Livestock Show
• End the day with fireworks

Who hosts it?

The Annual American Royal Barbecue contest is sanctioned by the Kansas City Barbecue Society.

Photos courtesy of American Royal Association

How do I get more information?

For more information, visit www.arbbq.com.

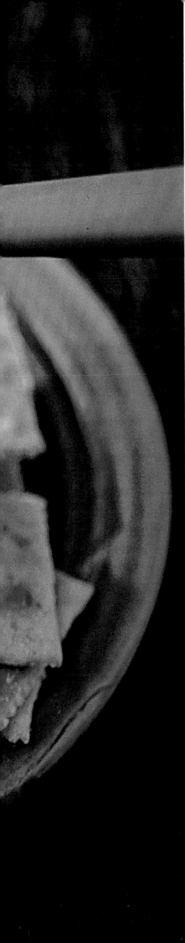

Brunswick Stew

To make this recipe thicker, cook it longer, being sure to stir it often.

Prep: 30 min.; **Soak:** 30 min.; **Grill:** 2 hr., 30 min. (chicken), 6 hr. (pork); **Cook:** 2 hr., 30 min.

Hickory wood chips

2 (2½-lb.) whole chickens

1 (3-lb.) Boston butt pork roast

3 (14½-oz.) cans diced tomatoes

2 (16-oz.) packages frozen whole kernel yellow corn, thawed

2 (16-oz.) packages frozen butterbeans, thawed

2 medium onions, chopped

1 (32-oz.) container chicken broth

1 (24-oz.) bottle ketchup

½ cup white vinegar

½ cup Worcestershire sauce

¼ cup firmly packed brown sugar

1 Tbsp. salt

1 Tbsp. pepper

2 Tbsp. hot sauce

Shopping tip: A 2 lb. smoked, cooked chicken and 2½ lb. smoked, cooked pork may be substituted for smoking the meats.

1. Soak wood chips in water for at least 30 minutes.
2. Prepare charcoal fire in smoker; let burn 15 to 20 minutes.
3. Drain wood chips, and place on coals. Place water pan in smoker; add water to depth of fill line.
4. Remove and discard giblets from chicken. Tuck wings under; tie with string, if desired. Place chicken and pork on lower food rack; cover with smoker lid.
5. Cook chicken 2½ hours; cook pork 6 hours or until a meat thermometer inserted into thickest portion registers 165°. Let cool.
6. Remove chicken from bone. Chop chicken and pork.
7. Stir together chicken, pork, diced tomatoes, corn, and remaining ingredients in a 6-qt. Dutch oven. Cover and simmer over low heat, stirring occasionally, 2½ to 3 hours. **Makes** 28 cups.

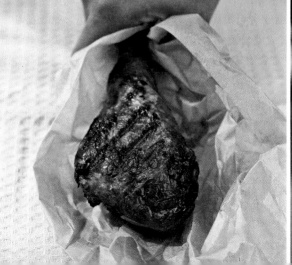

Old Hickory Bar-B-Que

Chopped Mutton	$1.75	Pickles	50¢
Chopped Pork	1.75	Chips	50¢
Burgoo	1.50		
Soft Drinks: 12oz- .75, 20oz- 1.25			

Speed
BBQ

Marinated Beef Kabobs With Vegetables

Cutting the roast into cubes and marinating it overnight tenderizes the meat and reduces the cooking time.

Prep: 27 min.; **Chill:** 8 hr.; **Grill:** 16 min.

1 cup white wine vinegar

1 cup vegetable oil

⅓ cup soy sauce

1 Tbsp. dried rosemary

1 Tbsp. dried thyme

1 tsp. dry mustard

1 tsp. salt

1 tsp. pepper

½ tsp. Worcestershire sauce

2 garlic cloves, pressed

1 (3½-lb.) eye of round roast, cut into 1½-inch cubes

12 small whole onions

1 lb. large whole mushrooms

2 green, red, or yellow bell peppers, cut into 1½-inch pieces

8 to 10 (12-inch) skewers

1. Stir together first 10 ingredients; reserve ½ cup marinade, and chill. Pour remaining marinade into a large zip-top plastic freezer bag. Add meat cubes; seal and chill 8 hours. Drain, discarding marinade.

2. Preheat grill to 350° to 400° (medium-high) heat. Thread meat and vegetables onto 12-inch skewers.

3. Grill, covered with grill lid, 16 minutes, basting with reserved marinade and turning often. **Makes** 8 to 10 servings.

Beef Fajitas With Pico de Gallo

Prep: 5 min.; **Chill:** 8 hr.; **Grill:** 13 min.; **Stand:** 5 min.

1 (8-oz.) bottle zesty Italian dressing

3 Tbsp. fajita seasoning

2 (1-lb.) flank steaks

12 (6-inch) flour tortillas, warmed

Shredded Cheddar cheese

Pico de Gallo

Garnishes: lime wedges, fresh cilantro sprigs

Shopping tip: We tested with McCormick Fajita Seasoning.

1. Combine Italian dressing and fajita seasoning in a shallow dish or zip-top plastic freezer bag; add steak. Cover or seal, and chill 8 hours, turning occasionally. Remove steak from marinade, discarding marinade.

2. Preheat grill to 350° to 400° (medium-high) heat. Grill steaks, covered with grill lid, 8 minutes. Turn and grill 5 more minutes or to desired degree of doneness. Remove steaks, and let stand 5 minutes.

3. Cut steaks diagonally across the grain into very thin slices; serve with tortillas, cheese, and Pico de Gallo. Garnish, if desired. **Makes** 6 servings.

Mexican Fiesta

Serves 6 hungry folks

Black bean salsa with chips

BEEF FAJITAS WITH PICO DE GALLO

MEXICAN RICE

Tequila Mojitos, page 212

Pico de Gallo

Prep: 25 min.; **Chill:** 1 hr.

1 pt. grape tomatoes, chopped

1 green bell pepper, chopped

1 red bell pepper, chopped

1 avocado, peeled and chopped

½ medium-size red onion, chopped

½ cup chopped fresh cilantro

1 garlic clove, pressed

¾ tsp. salt

½ tsp. ground cumin

½ tsp. lime zest

¼ cup fresh lime juice

1. Stir together all ingredients; cover and chill 1 hour. **Makes** about 3 cups.

Ingredient tip: Two large tomatoes, chopped, may be substituted for the grape tomatoes.

Flank Steak With Radish Salsa

Prep: 5 min.; **Grill:** 16 min.; **Stand:** 5 min.

1 (2-lb.) flank steak

1 Tbsp. Montreal steak seasoning

Radish Salsa

Shopping tip: We tested with McCormick Grill Mates Montreal Steak Seasoning.

1. Preheat grill to 350° to 400° (medium-high) heat. Sprinkle both sides of steak with seasoning. Grill steak, covered with grill lid, 8 minutes on each side or to desired degree of doneness. Remove from grill, and cover steak with aluminum foil; let stand 5 minutes. Uncover and cut steak diagonally across the grain into thin slices. Serve with Radish Salsa. **Makes** 6 servings.

Radish Salsa

This recipe easily doubles. Serve it over grilled burgers, spoon it into tacos, or offer it as an appetizer with tortilla chips.

Prep: 10 min.; **Chill:** 2 hr.

6 large radishes, grated

1 large cucumber, peeled, seeded, and chopped

¼ cup chopped fresh cilantro

1 garlic clove, pressed

1 Tbsp. fresh lime juice

¼ tsp. salt

1. Toss together all ingredients. Cover and chill up to 2 hours. Season with salt to taste. **Makes** about 2 cups.

tips for a tailgate

Flank steak is the perfect cut of beef for fajitas and a fun addition to burgers and brats at your tailgate. Transform this popular meat into a flavorful and juicy entrée by marinating it before game day, grilling it rare to medium rare, and slicing it across the grain into thin strips. Add your favorite fixins' and your "famous fajitas" will become an automatic crowd-pleaser.

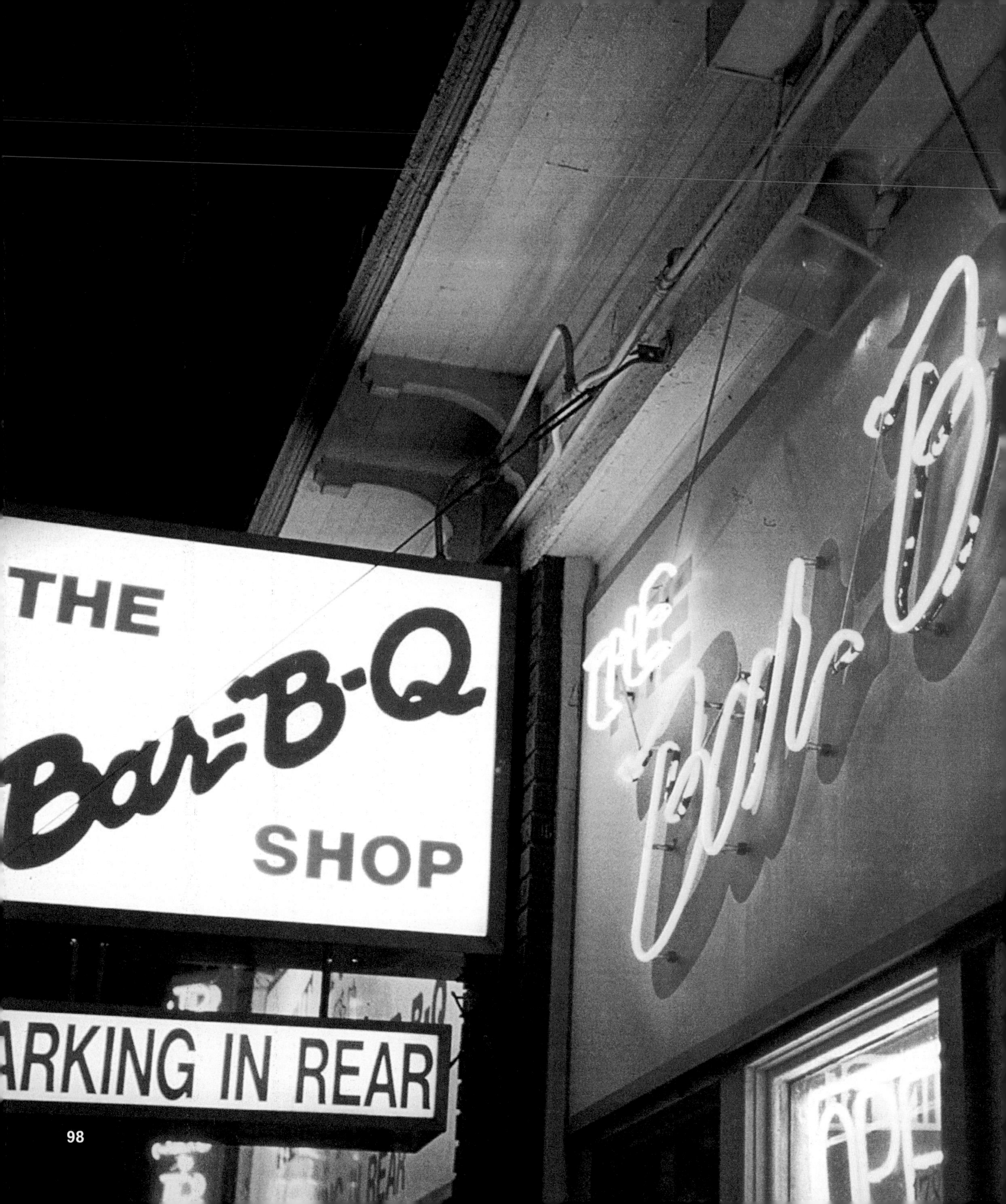
THE
Bar-B-Q
SHOP
ARKING IN REAR

Asian BBQ Flank Steak

Prep: 10 min.; **Chill:** 4 hr.; **Grill:** 10 min.; **Stand:** 10 min.

¼ cup lite soy sauce

3 Tbsp. lite teriyaki sauce

3 Tbsp. rice wine vinegar

1 Tbsp. Asian garlic-chili sauce

1 Tbsp. minced fresh ginger

2 green onions, chopped

1 (1½-lb.) flank steak

1. Combine soy sauce, teriyaki sauce, and next 4 ingredients in a large zip-top plastic freezer bag or shallow dish. Add steak, and turn to coat. Seal or cover, and chill 4 hours, turning occasionally.

2. Preheat grill to 350° to 400° (medium-high) heat. Remove steak from marinade, discarding marinade.

3. Grill flank steak, covered with grill lid, 5 to 7 minutes on each side or to desired degree of doneness. Let stand 10 minutes before slicing. Cut diagonally across the grain into thin strips. **Makes** 4 to 6 servings.

Grilled Tenderloin With Sautéed Mushrooms

Marjoram is added toward the end of cooking to retain its flavor.

Prep: 12 min.; **Stand:** 10 min.; **Cook:** 6 min.; **Grill:** 8 min.

4 garlic cloves, crushed

½ tsp. salt, divided

¾ tsp. freshly ground pepper, divided

6 beef tenderloin fillets (about 2 lb.)

1 Tbsp. vegetable oil

1½ lb. sliced fresh mushrooms

¼ cup butter, melted

2½ tsp. minced fresh sweet marjoram

¼ cup dry sherry

1. Preheat grill to 350° to 400° (medium-high) heat. Rub garlic, ¼ tsp. salt, and ½ tsp. pepper evenly over both sides of steaks; brush both sides with oil. Cover and let stand 10 minutes.

2. Cook mushrooms in butter in a large skillet over medium-high heat, stirring constantly, 1 minute. Stir in remaining ¼ tsp. salt and ¼ tsp. pepper, marjoram, and sherry; bring to a boil. Reduce heat, and simmer, uncovered, stirring occasionally, until mushrooms are tender and liquid is slightly reduced (about 5 to 7 minutes). Remove from heat; cover and keep warm.

3. Coat grill rack with cooking spray; place on grill. Place steaks on rack, and grill 4 minutes on each side or to desired degree of doneness. Serve mushrooms over steaks. **Makes** 6 servings.

'Que and A

Q: What's the difference between charcoal briquettes and hardwood lump charcoal? Is one better to use than the other?

A: Briquettes are the most common type of charcoal. They don't burn as hot as lump charcoal, which in turn means they last longer: about twice as long as hardwood lump charcoal. Use them when cooking low and slow for more consistency in temperature and longer burn time. A lot of briquettes have been soaked in lighter fluid, so you'll want to make sure to burn it all off before adding your food to the grill.

If things get any better, I may have to hire someone to help me enjoy it. Southern proverb

101

Virginia

Here's where to get great 'Q in the state.

The Smokey Pig
212 South Washington Highway
Ashland
(804) 798-4590
www.thesmokeypig.com

SHORT SUGAR'S
2215 Riverside Drive
Danville
(434) 793-4800

Allman's Pit Cooked Bar-B-Que
1299 Jeff Davis Highway
Fredericksburg
(540) 373-9881
www.allmansbarbeque.com

Eley's Barbeque
3221 West Washington Street
Petersburg
(804) 732-5861

PIERCE'S PITT BAR-B-QUE
447 East Rochambeau Drive
Williamsburg
(757) 565-2955
www.pierces.com

Chile-Rubbed Steak With Corn and Red Pepper Relish

For spicier steaks, increase the ground red pepper by ¼ tsp. or more.

Prep: 22 min.; **Grill:** 30 min; **Stand:** 10 min.

1 tsp. olive oil

3 ears corn

1 red bell pepper

½ cup finely chopped red onion

¼ cup finely chopped fresh cilantro

1 Tbsp. fresh lime juice

1 tsp. brown sugar

¾ tsp. salt, divided

½ tsp. onion powder

½ tsp. ground cumin

½ tsp. brown sugar

½ tsp. dried oregano

½ tsp. Spanish smoked paprika

¼ tsp. garlic powder

¼ tsp. ground red pepper

⅛ tsp. black pepper

6 (4-oz.) beef tenderloin fillets (about 1 inch thick)

1. Preheat grill to 350° to 400° (medium-high) heat.

2. Brush oil over corn and bell pepper. Place corn and bell pepper on grill rack coated with cooking spray; grill 20 minutes or until lightly browned, turning every 5 minutes. Place bell pepper in a zip-top plastic freezer bag; seal. Let stand 10 minutes. Remove pepper from bag; peel and chop. Place pepper in a large bowl.

3. Cut kernels from ears of corn to measure 2½ cups; add to bell pepper. Stir in onion, cilantro, lime juice, brown sugar, and ¼ tsp. salt; set relish aside.

4. Combine ½ tsp. salt, onion powder, and next 7 ingredients; rub salt mixture evenly over steaks. Place steaks on a grill rack coated with cooking spray; grill 5 minutes on each side or to desired degree of doneness. Serve with relish. **Makes** 6 servings.

tips from the pit master

Take the meat out of the refrigerator while the grill is heating, and let it stand for 30 to 45 minutes. Having the meat at room temperature is important because if you put it on the grill cold, the outer portion will burn.

Cilantro-Garlic Sirloin With Zesty Corn Salsa

Prep: 15 min.; **Chill:** 2 hr.; **Grill:** 20 min.; **Stand:** 10 min.

1 cup (1 bunch) fresh cilantro, packed

2 garlic cloves

3 Tbsp. fresh lime juice

1 Tbsp. lime zest

½ tsp. salt

½ tsp. ground cumin

¼ to ½ tsp. ground red pepper

2 lb. top sirloin steak (1¼ inches thick)

Zesty Corn Salsa

Garnish: fresh cilantro sprig

1. Process first 7 ingredients in a food processor or blender until blended, and rub cilantro mixture over sirloin steak. Chill 2 hours.

2. Preheat grill to 350° to 400° (medium-high) heat. Grill, covered with grill lid, 10 to 12 minutes on each side or to desired degree of doneness. Let stand 10 minutes.

3. Cut steak diagonally across the grain into thin strips. Serve with Zesty Corn Salsa; garnish, if desired. **Makes** 8 servings.

Zesty Corn Salsa

Prep: 15 min.; **Grill:** 20 min.

6 ears fresh corn, shucked

½ tsp. lime zest

¼ cup fresh lime juice

2 tsp. olive oil

1 small jalapeño pepper, minced

¼ tsp. salt

¼ tsp. ground cumin

1. Preheat grill to 350° to 400° (medium-high) heat. Grill corn, covered with grill lid, 10 minutes on each side or until browned on all sides. Remove from grill; cool.

2. Cut corn from cob into a bowl; stir in zest and remaining ingredients. **Makes** 4 cups.

Everybody thinks their sauce is "it," but as long as it's lip-smacking and finger-licking, it's good. If it's messy, it's wonderful. And that's all that matters.

Steak House-Marinated Sirloin Steak

Prep: 10 min.; **Chill:** 4 hr.; **Grill:** 8 min.; **Stand:** 10 min.

1 (1-lb.) boneless sirloin steak

Steak House-Style Marinade

½ tsp. salt

½ tsp. coarsely ground pepper

1. Pierce steak several times with a fork. Place Steak House-Style Marinade in a shallow dish or large zip-top plastic freezer bag; add steak. Cover or seal; chill at least 4 hours or up to 6 hours, turning occasionally.

2. Preheat grill to 350° to 400° (medium-high) heat.

3. Remove steak from marinade, discarding marinade. Pat steak dry, and sprinkle with salt and pepper.

4. Grill steak, covered with grill lid, 4 minutes on each side or to desired degree of doneness. Let stand 10 minutes before slicing. **Makes** 4 servings.

Steak House-Style Marinade

Length of marinating time depends on the size and cut of the beef. This amount of marinade will flavor a 1-lb. steak or three (1½-inch-thick) beef tenderloin fillets. Let stand 30 minutes at room temperature or 4 to 6 hours in the refrigerator to impart flavor, and then grill.

Prep: 10 min.

½ cup dark beer

2 Tbsp. olive oil

1 Tbsp. Worcestershire sauce

1 Tbsp. steak sauce

1 tsp. lemon zest

½ tsp. salt

¼ tsp. ground pepper

Shopping tip: We tested with A.1. Steak Sauce.

1. Whisk together beer and remaining ingredients until blended. Use immediately, or cover and chill until ready to use. Store in an airtight container in refrigerator up to 3 days. If chilled, let stand at room temperature 10 minutes before using. Whisk before using. **Makes** ¾ cup.

tools of the trade

Plastic bags: Large zip-top plastic freezer bags (in contrast to lighter weight food storage bags) provide an inexpensive and disposable container for marinating your goodies for the grill and storing leftovers. If your bag contains a lot of marinade, be sure to double-bag it. After marinating, discard the bag and marinade, or boil the marinade for at least 1 minute to kill any bacteria that may have been transferred from the raw food before using it to baste or to serve.

Dixie Beef Burgers With Chowchow Spread

Prep: 35 min.; **Grill:** 14 min.

½ cup chowchow

3 Tbsp. mayonnaise

1 (13.5-oz.) package frozen onion rings

1 cup grape tomatoes, quartered

1 Tbsp. honey

½ tsp. cider vinegar

½ cup finely chopped sweet onion, divided

¾ tsp. salt, divided

1½ lb. ground chuck

½ tsp. coarsely ground pepper

1 (8-oz.) package country ham biscuit slices

4 sourdough hamburger buns, split

4 green leaf lettuce leaves

Shopping tip: We tested with Alexia Onion Rings with panko coating and Braswell's Mild Chow Chow.

1. To prepare chowchow spread, stir together ½ cup chowchow and 3 Tbsp. mayonnaise in a small bowl. Cover and chill.

2. Preheat oven to 200°. Prepare onion rings according to package directions; keep warm on a wire rack in a jelly-roll pan at 200° up to 20 minutes.

3. Stir together tomatoes, honey, cider vinegar, ¼ cup onion, and ¼ tsp. salt.

4. Preheat grill to 350° to 400° (medium-high) heat. Gently combine beef, pepper, and remaining ¼ cup onion and ½ tsp. salt in a large bowl until blended. Shape mixture into 4 (4-inch wide, ¾-inch thick) patties.

5. Grill, covered with grill lid, 5 to 6 minutes on each side or until beef is no longer pink in center. Grill ham slices 1 to 2 minutes on each side or until lightly crisp. Grill buns, cut sides down, 1 to 2 minutes or until lightly toasted.

6. Layer each of 4 bun halves with lettuce, burger, chowchow spread, grilled ham slices, and an onion ring. Spoon tomato mixture into centers of each onion ring. Top with remaining bun halves. Serve with remaining onion rings. **Makes** 4 servings.

Steak House @ Home

Serves 4 hungry folks

MOLASSES GRILLED RIB-EYE STEAKS

Garlic Mashed Potatoes, page 249

Caesar salad or wedge salad

TOASTED BREAD WITH BUTTER

Molasses Grilled Rib-Eye Steaks

Prep: 10 min.; **Chill:** 2 hr.; **Grill:** 10 min.

½ cup molasses

¼ cup coarse-grained Dijon mustard

1 Tbsp. olive oil

4 (8- to 10-oz.) boneless beef rib-eye steaks

¾ tsp. salt

¾ tsp. pepper

1. Combine ½ cup molasses, ¼ cup mustard, and 1 Tbsp. olive oil in a shallow dish or large zip-top plastic freezer bag. Add steaks; cover or seal, and chill at least 2 hours, turning occasionally. Remove steaks from marinade, discarding marinade. Sprinkle steaks evenly with salt and pepper.

2. Preheat grill to 350° to 400° (medium-high) heat. Grill, covered with grill lid, 5 to 7 minutes on each side or to desired degree of doneness. **Makes** 4 servings.

Giant Barbecue Bacon Burger

Prep: 16 min.; **Cook:** 18 min.

2 Tbsp. butter

½ cup finely chopped onion

1½ lb. lean ground beef

⅓ cup quick-cooking oats

1 large egg

¼ cup barbecue sauce

¾ tsp. salt

⅛ tsp. pepper

6 bacon slices, cooked

4 (1-oz.) Cheddar cheese slices

1 (9-inch) round bread loaf, unsliced

¼ cup barbecue sauce

4 lettuce leaves

1 tomato, sliced

¼ cup dill pickle slices

1. Preheat grill to 350° to 400° (medium-high) heat. Place butter in a microwave-safe bowl. Cover with wax paper, and microwave at HIGH 30 seconds or until butter melts. Stir in onion. Cover and microwave at HIGH 2 more minutes or until onion is tender. Cool. Add beef, oats, egg, ¼ cut barbecue sauce, salt, and pepper; mix well. Turn beef mixture out onto a big piece of aluminum foil, and shape into a 9-inch patty.

2. Grill patty, covered with grill lid, 8 minutes on each side or until no longer pink, using a wide spatula to turn. Arrange bacon and cheese on patty the last 2 minutes of cooking.

3. Cut loaf of bread in half horizontally. Spread ¼ cup barbecue sauce over cut side of bottom half of bread. Arrange lettuce over barbecue sauce. Top with burger, tomato slices, and pickles. Cut burger into wedges to serve. **Makes** 6 servings.

tips for a tailgate

Burgers are always a hit at any tailgate. Top two tips for a perfect burger: Don't overwork the meat, and prevent a dome from forming as they cook by pressing a ½-inch indention in the center of each patty. Your burgers will grill up flat and fabulous.

Bluegrass & Barbecue Festival

Dillard, Georgia

Relax to the sound of bluegrass music as you catch up with family and friends and enjoy some delicious barbecue.

What is it?

A family fun event in the North Georgia mountains with barbecue, grits, cabbage, and dessert competitions.

What is there to do?

• Listen to bluegrass bands from all over the country

• Enjoy the company of friends and family as you camp throughout the weekend

Who hosts it?

The Dillard Bluegrass & Barbecue Festival is the Georgia State Championship Cook-off and is sanctioned by the Kansas City Barbecue Society.

How do I get more information?

Visit www.dillardbbq.org, or call (706) 746-2690.

Photos courtesy of Dillard Bluegrass Barbecue Festival

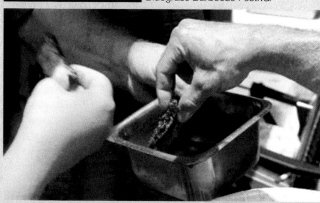

Bacon-Wrapped Barbecue Burgers

This dressed-up burger is a true crowd-pleaser. If you use ground beef from your freezer, make sure it has been well wrapped and frozen for three months or less to ensure best flavor.

Prep: 25 min.; **Cook:** 4 min.; **Chill:** 10 min.; **Grill:** 10 min.; **Stand:** 5 min.

8 bacon slices

1 (4.5-oz.) jar sliced mushrooms, drained and chopped

½ cup chopped Vidalia or sweet onion

2 tsp. olive oil

½ cup bottled honey barbecue sauce, divided

1½ lb. ground beef

¼ tsp. salt

4 sesame seed hamburger buns, toasted

Shopping tip: We tested with Kraft Honey Barbecue Sauce.

1. Arrange bacon on a paper towel-lined microwave-safe plate; cover with a paper towel. Microwave bacon at HIGH 2 minutes or until edges begin to crinkle and bacon is partially cooked.

2. Sauté mushrooms and onion in hot oil in a small nonstick skillet over medium heat 4 to 5 minutes or until tender and liquid is absorbed. Remove from heat, and stir in 2 Tbsp. barbecue sauce.

3. Preheat grill to 350° to 400° (medium-high) heat. Shape ground beef into 8 (5-inch) thin patties. Place 2 Tbsp. mushroom mixture in center of each of 4 patties. Top with remaining patties, pressing edges to seal. Shape into 4-inch patties. Wrap sides of each patty with 2 bacon slices, overlapping ends of each slice. Secure bacon using wooden picks. Sprinkle patties with salt. Cover and chill 10 minutes.

4. Grill patties, covered with grill lid, 5 to 6 minutes on 1 side. Turn and baste with half of remaining barbecue sauce. Grill 5 to 6 minutes or until beef is no longer pink in center. Turn and baste with remaining barbecue sauce. Remove from grill, and let stand 5 minutes. Remove wooden picks. Serve burgers on buns, and top with remaining mushroom mixture. **Makes** 4 servings.

tips from the pit master

Avoid pressing burger patties with a spatula as they grill. Pressing patties causes them to lose their tasty juices.

Herb-Marinated Pork Steaks

Prep: 15 min.; **Chill:** 2 hr.; **Grill:** 20 min.

1 (3½- to 4-lb.) boneless pork loin roast

1 small onion, chopped

2 garlic cloves, minced

½ cup vegetable oil

3 Tbsp. cider vinegar

1 Tbsp. lemon juice

1 tsp. dried oregano

½ tsp. dried rosemary

¼ tsp. dried dillweed

¼ tsp. salt

¼ tsp. pepper

Garnishes: flat-leaf parsley sprigs, lemon halves

Shopping tip: We tested with Crisco Pure Vegetable Oil. Eight (1-inch-thick) boneless pork chops may be substituted.

1. Cut roast into 6 to 8 (1-inch-thick) pieces, and place in a large shallow dish or large zip-top plastic freezer bag.

2. Stir together chopped onion, minced garlic, and next 8 ingredients; pour over pork. Cover or seal, and chill at least 2 hours, turning occasionally. Remove pork from marinade, discarding marinade.

3. Preheat grill to 350 to 400 (medium-high) heat. Grill pork, covered with grill lid, 20 minutes or until a meat thermometer inserted into thickest portion registers 155°, turning once. Remove from grill, and let stand until meat thermometer registers 160°. Garnish, if desired. **Makes** 6 to 8 servings.

Kentucky

Here's where to get great 'Q in the state.

Carr's Barn
216 West Broadway Street
Mayfield
(270) 247-8959

HILL'S BAR-B-QUE
1002 Cuba Road
Mayfield
(270) 247-9121
www.hills4bbq.com

MOONLITE BAR-B-Q INN
2840 West Parrish Avenue
Owensboro
(270) 684-8143 or
1-800-322-8989
www.moonlite.com

Old Hickory Bar-B-Que
338 Washington Avenue
Owensboro
(270) 926-9000

OLE SOUTH BBQ
3523 State 54 East
Owensboro
(270) 926-6464

D. STARNES BAR-B-Q
1008 Joe Clifton Drive
Paducah
(270) 444-9555

"A KENTUCKY TRADITION."
MOONLITE
BBQ INN
OWENSBORO, KY
Bar-B-Q Capitol of the World!

Spicy Grilled Pork Tenderloin

Caribbean seasoning adds a touch of sweet heat to these grilled tenderloins. If you're in search of an easy entrée that can go from everyday to gourmet, this is it.

Prep: 5 min.; **Grill:** 20 min.; **Stand:** 10 min.

---

2 lb. pork tenderloins

1 Tbsp. olive oil

1½ Tbsp. Caribbean jerk seasoning

Shopping tip: We tested with McCormick Caribbean Jerk Seasoning.

1. Preheat grill to 350° to 400° (medium-high) heat. Brush tenderloins with olive oil, and rub evenly with seasoning.

2. Grill, covered with grill lid, 10 minutes on each side or until a meat thermometer inserted in the thickest portion registers 155°. Remove from grill, and let stand 10 minutes. **Makes** 6 servings.

Grilled Honey-Mustard Pork Tenderloin

Prep: 10 min.; **Chill:** 2 hr.; **Grill:** 20 min.; **Stand:** 10 min.

½ cup chopped fresh parsley

½ cup red wine vinegar

¼ cup olive oil

¼ cup honey

3 Tbsp. country-Dijon mustard

2 garlic cloves, minced

1 Tbsp. kosher salt

1½ tsp. coarsely ground pepper

2½ lb. pork tenderloins

1. Stir together chopped parsley and next 7 ingredients until blended. Pour mixture in a large shallow dish or zip-top plastic freezer bag; add pork, cover or seal, and chill at least 2 hours or up to 8 hours, turning occasionally. Remove pork, discarding marinade.

2. Preheat grill to 350° to 400° (medium-high) heat. Grill tenderloin, covered with grill lid, 10 minutes on each side or until a meat thermometer inserted into thickest portion registers 155°. Remove tenderloin from grill, and let stand 10 minutes before slicing. **Makes** 8 servings.

'Que and A

Q: I know pork is done at 160°. Why do some recipes say to cook it to 190°?

A: While pork is safe to eat at 160°, some cuts are more flavorful and tender at a higher temperature. Typically leaner cuts like pork tenderloin and pork chops are best cooked at the lower end. You may see recipes calling to cook the pork until 150° to 155° and letting it stand. This accounts for carryover heat that will raise the internal temperature to 160° and thus prevent overcooking. Fattier cuts of pork, such as Boston butts, will be tenderer at a higher temperature.

Grilled Pork Tenderloin With Gingered Jezebel Sauce

Prep: 10 min.; **Chill:** 20 min.; **Grill:** 25 min.; **Stand:** 10 min.

½ cup lite soy sauce

2 Tbsp. dark brown sugar

2 green onions, chopped

2 Tbsp. sherry (optional)

3 lb. pork tenderloins

1¼ Gingered Jezebel Sauce

Garnish: fresh rosemary

1. Combine first 3 ingredients and, if desired, sherry in a shallow dish or large zip-top plastic freezer bag; add pork. Cover or seal, and chill 20 minutes.
2. Preheat grill to 350° to 400° (medium-high) heat. Remove pork from marinade, discarding marinade. Grill pork, covered with grill lid, 25 minutes or until a meat thermometer inserted into thickest portion registers 155°, turning once and basting with ½ cup Gingered Jezebel Sauce the last 5 to 10 minutes. Let stand 10 minutes or until thermometer registers 160°. Slice and serve with remaining ¾ cup Gingered Jezebel Sauce. Garnish, if desired. **Makes** 8 servings.

Gingered Jezebel Sauce

Ginger replaces dry mustard in this version of Jezebel sauce.

Cook: 2 min.

⅔ cup pineapple preserves

⅓ cup apple jelly

2 Tbsp. prepared horseradish

1 Tbsp. grated fresh ginger

1. Microwave pineapple preserves and apple jelly in a glass bowl at HIGH 2 minutes or until melted. Stir in remaining ingredients. **Makes** 1¼ cups.

Barbecue festivals celebrate more than just great food. Grab some friends and enjoy the fun.

Mixed Grill With Cilantro Pesto

Prep: 5 min.; **Grill:** 16 min. (chops), 13 min. (fillet); **Stand:** 5 min.

4 (1½-inch-thick) center-cut bone-in pork chops

4 (6-oz.) beef tenderloin fillets (about 2 inches thick)

Kosher salt

Pepper

Cilantro Pesto

1. Sprinkle pork chops and beef fillets evenly with desired amount of salt and pepper.
2. Grill chops and fillets, covered with grill lid, over medium-high heat (350° to 400°). Grill chops 8 to 10 minutes on each side or until done. Grill fillets 8 to 10 minutes. Turn fillets over, and cook 5 more minutes or to desired degree of doneness. Remove chops and fillets from grill, and let stand 5 minutes. Serve with Cilantro Pesto. **Makes** 8 servings.

Cilantro Pesto

This pesto has a rougher, drier consistency than traditional ones. For a saucier version, simply add more olive oil. Try it with grilled chicken, fish, or veggies in addition to pork and beef.

Prep: 10 min.

½ cup loosely packed fresh cilantro leaves

½ cup loosely packed fresh flat-leaf parsley

2 garlic cloves

¼ cup (1 oz.) freshly grated Parmesan cheese

2 Tbsp. pumpkin seeds, toasted

¼ tsp. salt

¼ cup olive oil

1. Pulse first 6 ingredients in a food processor 10 times or just until chopped. Drizzle olive oil over mixture, and pulse 6 more times or until a coarse mixture forms. Cover and chill until ready to serve. **Makes** about ¾ cup.

Comfort Food Menu

Serves 6 hungry folks

GRILLED MAPLE CHIPOTLE PORK CHOPS

Smoked Gouda Grits, page 249

Buttered green beans

NUTTER BUTTER® BANANA PUDDING TRIFLE (PAGE 280)

Grilled Maple Chipotle Pork Chops on Smoked Gouda Grits

We adapted this recipe from one of the finalists in our 2002 Cook-Off.

Prep: 10 min.; **Grill:** 20 min.

½ cup barbecue sauce

½ cup maple syrup

2 chipotle peppers in adobo sauce, seeded and minced

1 tsp. adobo sauce from can

6 (1¼-inch-thick) bone-in pork loin chops

1 tsp. salt

1 tsp. pepper

Smoked Gouda Grits (see page 249)

1. Preheat grill to 350° to 400° (medium-high) heat. Whisk together first 4 ingredients, and set aside.

2. Sprinkle pork chops evenly with salt and pepper.

3. Grill, covered with grill lid, 20 minutes or until a meat thermometer inserted into thickest portion registers 155°, turning once. Baste with half of barbecue sauce mixture the last 5 minutes of cooking or when meat thermometer registers 145°.

4. Spoon Smoked Gouda Grits evenly onto 6 serving plates; top each with a pork chop, and drizzle evenly with remaining barbecue sauce mixture. **Makes** 6 servings.

Grilled Pork Chops With Garlic Mashed Potatoes

Prep: 10 min.; **Grill:** 10 min.

¼ cup olive oil

1 Tbsp. salt

1 Tbsp. chopped fresh or dried rosemary

1 Tbsp. chopped fresh thyme

2 Tbsp. chopped fresh oregano

1 Tbsp. coarsely ground pepper

8 (12-oz.) bone-in pork loin chops

Garlic Mashed Potatoes (see page 249)

Garnish: fresh thyme sprigs

Shopping tip: 8 (12-oz.) bone-in veal chops may be substituted for the pork loin chops

1. Preheat grill to 350° to 400° (medium-high) heat. Stir together first 6 ingredients. Rub evenly over both sides of pork chops.

2. Grill, covered with grill lid, over medium-high heat (350° to 400°) 10 to 12 minutes or until meat thermometer inserted into thickest portion registers 155°, turning once. Serve with Garlic Mashed Potatoes. Garnish, if desired. **Makes** 8 servings.

Grilled Basil-and-Garlic Pork Chops

Prep: 5 min.; **Grill:** 10 min.

1 tsp. salt

1 tsp. pepper

1 tsp. dried basil

½ tsp. garlic powder

6 (6- to 8-oz.) bone-in pork loin chops

1. Preheat grill to 350° to 400° (medium-high) heat. Combine first 4 ingredients; sprinkle over pork chops.

2. Grill pork, covered with grill lid, over 350° to 400° (medium-high) heat 5 to 7 minutes on each side or until done. **Makes** 6 servings.

Jalapeño-Basil Pork Chops

Prep: 10 min.; **Cook:** 5 min.; **Stand:** 30 min.; **Grill:** 6 min.

1 (10-oz.) jar jalapeño pepper jelly

½ cup dry white wine

¼ cup chopped fresh basil

4 (1-inch-thick) bone-in pork loin chops

½ tsp. salt

¼ tsp. pepper

1. Preheat grill to 350° to 400° (medium-high) heat. Cook first 3 ingredients in a small saucepan over low heat, stirring often, 5 minutes or until pepper jelly melts. Remove from heat, and let mixture cool completely.

2. Pour ¾ cup pepper jelly mixture into a large zip-top plastic freezer bag, reserving remaining mixture. Add pork chops, turning to coat. Seal and let stand at room temperature 30 minutes, turning pork chops occasionally.

3. Remove chops from marinade, discarding marinade. Sprinkle evenly with salt and pepper.

4. Grill, covered with grill lid, 3 to 4 minutes on each side or until a meat thermometer inserted into thickest portion registers 155°. Serve with remaining pepper jelly mixture. **Makes** 4 servings.

tools of the trade

Thermometers: Two types of thermometers are helpful for grilling. The first is a grill thermometer, which is typically included on gas grills. This thermometer tells the temperature inside the grill. If using a charcoal grill, look for a thermometer with a dial face and a long stem. The second helpful thermometer is an instant-read meat thermometer to help quickly determine doneness of meats. Be careful though—regular dial-faced instant-read thermometers are not heat resistant, so the can't be left in the meat for prolonged periods of time while grilling. A digital instant read with a probe solves this problem and tends to be more accurate.

Alabama

Here's where to get great 'Q in the state.

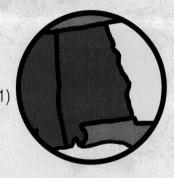

Green's Bar-B-Q Pit
27517 U.S. 29
Andalusia
(334) 388-2550

WHITT'S BARBECUE
1397 East Elm Street
Athens
(256) 232-7928

Mike & Ed's Bar-B-Q
307 North College Street
Auburn
(334) 501-1866

BOB SYKE'S BAR B-Q
1724 Ninth Avenue North
Bessemer
(205) 426-1400 or
www.bobsykes.com

JOHNNY RAY'S
3431 Colonnade Parkway
Birmingham
(205) 967-0099

THE ORIGINAL GOLDEN RULE
1571 Montgomery Highway
Birmingham
(205) 823-7770

Big Bob Gibson Bar-B-Q
1715 Sixth Avenue SE. (U.S. 31)
Decatur
(256) 350-6969
www.bigbobgibsonbbq.com

Perk's Bar-B-Que
41 Kelly Hill Circle
Harpersville
(205) 672-8533

Archibald's Bar-B-Q
1211 Martin Luther King Blvd.
Northport
(205) 345-6861

CHUCK'S BAR-B-QUE
905 Short Avenue
Opelika
(334) 749-4043

Dreamland Bar-B-Que
5535 15th Avenue East
Tuscaloosa
(205) 758-8135
www.dreamlandbbq.com

Spice-Rubbed Pork Chops With Summertime Salsa

Be sure to try the Summertime Salsa over grilled fish or steak. It's also great served with your favorite chips or ice cream.

Prep: 20 min.; **Grill:** 10 min.

¼ cup orange juice

2 tsp. chopped fresh mint

1 tsp. balsamic vinegar

½ tsp. ground cinnamon

2 large peaches, peeled and cubed (about 2 cups)

3 Tbsp. pork rub

6 (1-inch-thick) boneless pork chops

1 cup fresh raspberries

Garnish: fresh mint sprigs

Shopping tip: We tested with McCormick Grill Mates Pork Rub.

1. Preheat grill to 300° to 350° (medium) heat. Stir together first 4 ingredients in a medium bowl. Add peaches, tossing to coat.

2. Coat both sides of pork chops evenly with pork rub.

3. Grill, covered with grill lid, 5 to 7 minutes on each side or until a meat thermometer inserted into thickest portion registers 155°. Gently toss raspberries with peach mixture, and serve with pork chops. Garnish, if desired. **Makes** 6 servings.

tools of the trade

Timer: A kitchen timer can help prevent over-cooking and is especially helpful if grilling takes several hours and you're busy working on other parts of the meal. Keep it in the kitchen, by the grill, or wherever you're most likely to be. Stash it in a pocket if you'll be busy both indoors and outdoors.

Zesty Grilled Pork Chops

Prep: 10 min.; **Grill:** 6 min.

2 tsp. Creole seasoning

2 tsp. ground cumin

2 tsp. garlic powder

2 medium-size yellow squash, cut lengthwise into ¼-inch-thick slices

2 medium zucchini, cut lengthwise into ¼-inch-thick slices

2 Tbsp. olive oil, divided

6 (1¼-inch-thick) bone-in pork chops

1. Preheat grill to 400° to 500° (high) heat. Combine first 3 ingredients in a small bowl.

2. Toss squash and zucchini with 1 Tbsp. oil in a large bowl; sprinkle vegetables with 1 tsp. Creole mixture.

3. Stir remaining 1 Tbsp. oil into remaining Creole mixture. Rub evenly on pork chops.

4. Grill vegetables and pork chops 3 minutes on each side or until a meat thermometer inserted into thickest portion of pork chops registers 155°. **Makes** 6 servings.

Cane Pole Kabobs

Martha Foose and her husband, Donald Bender, who own Mockingbird Bakery in Greenwood, Mississippi, like to entertain friends in their home with these casual kabobs.

Prep: 25 min.; **Soak:** 30 min.; **Grill:** 9 min.

13 (12-inch) wooden or metal skewers

1 (16-oz.) package smoked sausage, cut into 2-inch pieces

1 (16-oz.) jar marinated cherry peppers, drained

2 medium-size sweet onions, quartered

1 cup barbecue sauce

1. Preheat grill to 300° to 350° (medium) heat. Soak wooden skewers in water 30 minutes to prevent burning.
2. Thread sausage, peppers, and onion quarters evenly onto skewers.
3. Grill, covered with grill lid, 4 to 6 minutes or until sausage is lightly browned. Turn and grill 3 more minutes; brush with barbecue sauce, and grill 2 more minutes. Serve with additional barbecue sauce, if desired. **Makes** 6 to 8 servings.

Grilled Sausages

Prep: 10 min.; **Cook:** 10 min.; **Stand:** 10 min.; **Grill:** 16 min.

4 fresh pork sausages

2 (12-oz.) bottles lager beer

2 (8-inch) hoagie rolls

Sweet Pepper-Onion Relish

Shopping tip: You may substitute chicken for the pork sausages. We tested with Johnsonville Stadium Style Brats and Yuengling Traditional Lager, but you may use 4½ cups water for the beer instead if you prefer.

1. Preheat grill to 350° to 400° (medium-high) heat. Bring sausages and beer to a boil in a Dutch oven over medium-high heat. Cover, remove from heat, and let stand 10 minutes. Drain.

2. Cut a ½-inch-deep wedge from top of each roll. Reserve wedges for another use, if desired. Cut rolls in half crosswise.

3. Grill sausages, covered with grill lid, 8 to 10 minutes on each side or to desired degree of doneness.

4. Place 1 sausage in each roll half. Spoon desired amount of Sweet Pepper-Onion Relish over each sausage. **Makes** 4 servings.

Sweet Pepper-Onion Relish

This relish also tastes great on grilled chicken or pork. For a tasty appetizer, serve with sliced rounds of French bread and a soft, creamy cheese.

Prep: 20 min.; **Bake:** 45 min.; **Cool:** 30 min.

2 red bell peppers, seeded and diced

2 yellow bell peppers, seeded and diced

1 large yellow onion, diced

3 garlic cloves, minced

2 Tbsp. olive oil

2 Tbsp. balsamic vinegar

1 tsp. salt

½ tsp. dried thyme

½ tsp. dried crushed red pepper

1. Preheat oven to 400°. Stir together all ingredients, and pour into an 11- x 7-inch baking dish. Bake 45 minutes or until soft, stirring every 5 minutes. Transfer pepper mixture and any liquid to a bowl. Let cool 30 minutes or to room temperature. Store in an airtight container in refrigerator up to 3 days. **Makes** 5 cups.

Super Bowl Party

Serves 8 hungry folks

Dixie Caviar, page 216

Barbecue Bean Dip, page 219

Special Deviled Eggs, page 237

HONEY-SOY APPETIZER RIBS, PAGE 56

GRILLED SAUSAGES (DOUBLE RECIPE)

Tangy Venison and Vegetables

Prep: 20 min.; **Chill:** 4 hr.; **Cook:** 10 min.; **Grill:** 15 min.

1½ lb. boneless venison
sirloin, cut into 1¼-inch cubes

½ cup red wine vinegar

¼ cup honey

¼ cup soy sauce

2 Tbsp. ketchup

Dash of garlic powder

Dash of pepper

12 small round red potatoes

1 large onion, cut into
6 wedges

1 medium zucchini, cut into
1-inch pieces

1 medium-size green pepper,
cut into 1½-inch pieces

12 fresh mushrooms

12 cherry tomatoes

6 (15-inch) metal skewers

1. Place venison in a zip-top plastic freezer bag. Combine vinegar and next 5 ingredients in a bowl; stir well. Set ¼ cup marinade aside. Pour remaining marinade over venison. Seal bag; marinate in refrigerator 4 hours, turning occasionally.

2. Cook potatoes in boiling water to cover 10 minutes; drain. One hour before grilling, combine potatoes, ¼ cup reserved marinade, onion, and next 4 ingredients; toss gently.

3. Preheat grill to 350° to 400° (medium-high) heat. Remove venison from marinade, reserving marinade. Bring marinade to a boil in a small saucepan; set aside. Alternately thread venison and vegetables onto six 15-inch metal skewers. Grill, covered with grill lid, 15 minutes or to desired degree of doneness, turning and basting occasionally with reserved marinade. **Makes** 6 servings.

'Que and A

Q: I've tried to grill kabobs before but the meat and vegetables always cook so unevenly. What am I doing wrong?

A: The most important thing to remember with kabobs is to cut the meat and vegetables so that they are the same size and will cook evenly. You can also thread the meat and veggies on separate skewers and remove them as they are done. Also, don't overcrowd your kabob ingredients—a little space when grilling will promote even heat.

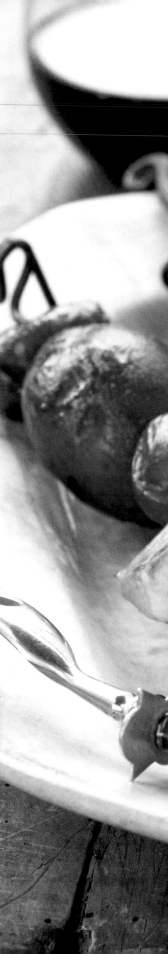

Memphis in May

Memphis, Tennessee

Make no bones about it, Memphis in May is serious business in the barbecue world.

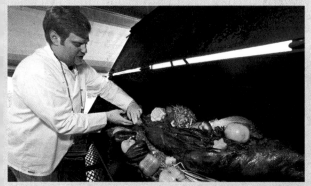

What is it?
A collection of more than 200 barbecue teams that have risen through the ranks by winning another sanctioned event throughout the South and nearly perfecting the art of smoking pork shoulders, ribs, or whole hogs.

What is there to do?
• Enjoy the Ms. Piggie competition, where grown men dress in tutus and snouts
• Visit the People's Choice tent where you can be a judge and sample world-class barbecue
• Enjoy music and fireworks while you take in the sounds, sights, and smells of Tom Lee Park

Who hosts it?
Memphis in May International Festival Inc., a 501-C(3), not-for-profit, community-based organization, hosts Memphis in May Barbecue Cooking Contest each year in Tom Lee Park in downtown Memphis.

How do I get more information?
Visit www.memphisinmay.org, or call (901) 525-4611.

Photos courtesy of Memphis in May International Festival, Inc.

Grilled Venison With Fennel Rub

Try this simple dish for your next cookout. Serve alongside roasted carrots, onions, red peppers, and potatoes.

Prep: 20 min.; **Grill:** 12 min.; **Stand:** 10 min.

2 tsp. fennel seeds

1 tsp. black peppercorns

½ tsp. salt

½ tsp. garlic powder

1 (1-lb.) venison tenderloin

Cooking spray

Shopping tip: If you don't have venison, substitute elk or beef tenderloin medallions.

1. Preheat grill to 350° to 400° (medium-high) heat.

2. Grind fennel and peppercorns with a mortar and pestle. Add salt and garlic powder. Rub fennel mixture over venison.

3. Place venison on grill rack coated with cooking spray; grill 12 minutes or until meat thermometer inserted into thickest part of meat registers 160°, turning occasionally. Let stand 10 minutes. Cut venison diagonally across grain into thin slices. **Makes** 4 servings.

tools of the trade

Grill Brush: A heavy-duty grill brush is a must for keeping your grill grates clean and helping prevent food from sticking to the grill. Look for stiff wire brushes, and remember that it's easier to clean up your mess before the grill cools. If you forget, cover the grates with heavy-duty foil while preheating, and then scrape the grates clean.

Barbecued Duck With Sweet-and-Sour Cabbage

Prep: 13 min.; **Cook:** 20 min; **Grill:** 14 min.; **Stand:** 5 min.

1 small onion, chopped

1 Tbsp. olive oil

8 cups thinly sliced red cabbage (about 1¼ lb.)

⅓ cup firmly packed brown sugar

2 Tbsp. cider vinegar

½ tsp. salt

¼ tsp. pepper

2 (14-oz.) packages boneless whole duck breasts, thawed

½ cup barbecue sauce

1. Preheat grill to 300° to 350° (medium) heat. Sauté onion in hot oil in a large skillet 5 minutes or until tender. Add cabbage, brown sugar, vinegar, salt, and pepper. Cover and cook 15 to 20 minutes or until cabbage is tender, stirring occasionally.

2. Grill duck breasts 8 minutes; baste with barbecue sauce. Turn and grill 6 to 8 minutes or until meat thermometer inserted into thickest part of breast registers 170° or desired doneness, basting occasionally. Let stand 5 minutes.

3. Remove skin from breasts. Slice each breast in half, and cut each half into ½-inch slices. Serve with cabbage. **Makes** 4 servings.

For extra spice, use two jalapeño peppers instead of one.

Prep: 25 min.; **Chill:** 8 hr.; **Grill:** 45 min.; **Stand:** 10 min.

½ cup coarsely chopped onion

6 green onions, sliced

2 garlic cloves, chopped

1 jalapeño pepper, coarsely chopped

2 Tbsp. brown sugar

4½ Tbsp. Jamaican jerk seasoning, divided

¾ cup mayonnaise

1 (3½-lb.) cut-up whole chicken

¼ tsp. salt

¼ tsp. pepper

Shopping tip: We tested with Hellman's and Best Foods Real Mayonnaise.

1. Process first 5 ingredients and 3 Tbsp. jerk seasoning in a food processor 15 seconds or until blended, using the metal blade. Add mayonnaise, and pulse 5 times or until blended.
2. Rub mayonnaise mixture over chicken. Cover and chill 8 to 24 hours.
3. Light 1 side of grill, heating to 400° to 450° (high) heat; leave other side unlit. Sprinkle chicken with salt, pepper, and remaining 1½ Tbsp. jerk seasoning. Place chicken over unlit side of grill, and grill, covered with grill lid, 45 minutes to 1 hour or until a meat thermometer inserted into thigh registers 170°. Transfer chicken to a serving platter; cover loosely with aluminum foil, and let stand 10 minutes before serving. **Makes** 6 servings.

Plum Good Chicken Fajitas

Prep: 15 min.; **Cook:** 3 min.; **Grill:** 14 min.; **Stand:** 5 min.

Plum Sauce (opposite page)

1 red bell pepper, cut into strips

1 green bell pepper, cut into strips

1 large red onion, sliced

2 Tbsp. olive oil

2 lb. skinned and boned chicken breasts

8 (8-inch) flour tortillas, warmed

Lime wedges

Toppings: guacamole, pico de gallo

1. Prepare Plum Sauce as directed. Remove and reserve 1 cup for basting. Keep remaining sauce warm.

2. Sauté bell peppers and onion in hot oil in a large skillet over medium-high heat 3 minutes or until crisp-tender. Keep warm.

3. Preheat grill to 350° to 400° (medium-high) heat. Grill chicken 7 minutes on each side or until a meat thermometer registers 165, basting often with 1 cup reserved Plum Sauce. Remove from grill and let stand 5 minutes.

4. Cut chicken into thin strips. Serve with sautéed vegetables, remaining Plum Sauce, warm tortillas, lime wedges, and desired toppings. **Makes** 8 servings.

Plum Sauce

Prep: 15 min.; **Cook:** 20 min.

1 Tbsp. butter

1 small onion, chopped

1 (7.6-oz.) jar Asian plum sauce

½ (6-oz.) can frozen lemonade concentrate

½ cup chili sauce

¼ cup soy sauce

1 Tbsp. dry mustard

1 tsp. ground ginger

1 tsp. Worcestershire sauce

¼ tsp. hot sauce

1. Melt butter in a medium saucepan over medium-high heat; add chopped onion, and sauté until tender. Stir in plum sauce and remaining ingredients. Bring sauce to a boil; reduce heat, and simmer 15 minutes.
Makes about 2 cups.

Cuban Mojo Chicken

Prep: 10 min.; **Stand:** 25 min.; **Grill:** 8 min.; **Cook:** 2 min.

¼ cup fresh orange juice

¼ cup fresh lime juice

2 garlic cloves, minced

1 tsp. ground cumin

½ tsp. dried oregano, crushed

½ tsp. paprika

½ tsp. salt

4 (5-oz.) boneless, skinless chicken breasts

1. Stir together first 7 ingredients in a shallow bowl or zip-top plastic freezer bag; add chicken. Cover and seal, and let stand 20 minutes. Remove chicken from marinade, reserving marinade. Pat chicken dry with paper towels.
2. Preheat grill to 300° to 350° (medium) heat. Grill, covered, 4 to 5 minutes on each side or until a meat thermometer registers 165°. Remove from grill and let stand 5 minutes.
3. Bring reserved marinade to a boil over medium-high heat. Boil 2 minutes, stirring often. Serve chicken with warm marinade. **Makes** 4 servings.

Meat & Three Menu

Serves 8 hungry folks

LEXINGTON-STYLE GRILLED CHICKEN

Fried Green Tomatoes With Bread-and-Butter Pickle Rémoulade, page 253

Grilled Okra and Tomato Skewers, page 254

FAVORITE MAC AND CHEESE

Lexington-Style Grilled Chicken

Larry Elder says Lexington, North Carolina, pork barbecue inspired him to create this spicy-hot vinegar marinade for chicken.

Prep: 15 min.; **Chill:** 2 hr.; **Grill:** 35 min.

2 cups cider vinegar

¼ cup firmly packed dark brown sugar

¼ cup vegetable oil

3 Tbsp. dried crushed red pepper

4 tsp. salt

2 tsp. pepper

2 (2½- to 3-lb.) cut-up whole chickens

1. Stir together first 6 ingredients until blended.

2. Place half each of vinegar mixture and chicken in a large zip-top plastic freezer bag; seal. Repeat procedure with remaining vinegar mixture and chicken, placing in a separate zip-top plastic freezer bag. Chill chicken at least 2 hours or up to 8 hours, turning occasionally.

3. Preheat grill to 350° to 400° (medium-high) heat. Remove chicken from marinade, discarding marinade. Grill chicken, covered with grill lid, 35 to 40 minutes or until meat thermometer inserted into breast registers 165°, and into thigh registers 170°, turning occasionally. **Makes** 8 to 10 servings.

Easy Barbecue Chicken

Prep: 12 min.; **Cook:** 36 min.; **Grill:** 35 min.

1 onion, chopped

1 garlic clove, minced

3 Tbsp. vegetable oil

1 cup ketchup

3 Tbsp. brown sugar

1 tsp. Worcestershire sauce

1 tsp. dry mustard

¼ tsp. pepper

⅓ cup fresh lemon juice

2 (2½- to 3-lb.) cut-up whole chickens

1. Sauté onion and garlic in hot oil in a medium saucepan over medium-high heat until onion begins to brown, about 6 minutes. Stir in 1 cup water, ketchup, brown sugar, Worcestershire sauce, mustard, and pepper. Bring to a boil; reduce heat, and simmer, stirring 30 minutes. Stir in lemon juice. Remove from heat, and set aside.

2. Preheat grill to 350° to 400° (medium-high) heat. Grill chicken, covered with grill lid, 35 to 40 minutes or until a meat thermometer inserted into breast registers 165° and into thigh registers 170°, turning chicken occasionally and basting frequently with sauce after 20 minutes. **Makes** 8 to 10 servings.

Grilled Garlic Chicken

Prep: 15 min.; **Chill:** 1 hr.; **Cook:** 35 min.

2 (3½-lb.) cut-up whole chickens

1 bunch green onions, minced

6 garlic cloves, minced

2 cups orange juice

¼ cup cider vinegar

2 tsp. dried oregano

2 tsp. kosher salt

½ tsp. crushed red pepper flakes

1. Place chicken pieces in 1 or 2 large zip-top plastic freezer bags, and add remaining ingredients. Shake to mix. Refrigerate at least 1 hour or overnight. Remove chicken from marinade; discard marinade.

2. Preheat grill to 350° to 400° (medium-high) heat. Grill chicken, covered with grill lid, 35 to 40 minutes or until a meat thermometer inserted into breast registers 165° and into thigh registers 170°, turning occasionally. **Makes** 8 to 10 servings.

Chicken With Grilled Green Onions

Prep: 30 min.; **Chill:** 30 min.; **Grill:** 12 min.

1 tsp. salt

½ tsp. pepper

2 Tbsp. olive oil

2 Tbsp. lime zest

3 Tbsp. fresh lime juice

4 bunches green onions

4 skinned and boned chicken breasts

1. Preheat grill to 350° to 400° (medium-high) heat. Process first 5 ingredients in a blender or food processor until smooth.

2. Place green onions in a shallow dish or zip-top plastic freezer bag; pour lime juice mixture over green onions. Cover or seal, and chill 30 minutes, turning occasionally.

3. Remove green onions from marinade, reserving marinade; set aside.

4. Grill chicken, covered with grill lid, 6 minutes on each side or until done, basting frequently with reserved marinade. Grill green onions, covered, 3 to 5 minutes on each side or until browned. Serve with grilled chicken. **Makes** 4 servings.

Florida

Here's where to get great 'Q in the state.

King's Taste Barbecue

503 Palmetto Street
Eustis
(352) 589-0404

Brodus' Bar-B-Que

103 Taylor Avenue
Groveland
(352) 429-4707

JACK BENNY'S BARBEQUE

100 South U.S. 27
Minneola
(352) 394-2673

BUBBALOU'S BODACIOUS BAR-B-QUE

12100 Challenger Parkway
Orlando
(407) 423-1212
www.bubbalous.com

BC's General Store

8730 County Road 48
Yalaha
(352) 324-3730

Margarita-Marinated Chicken With Mango Salsa

Prep: 10 min.; **Chill:** 2 hr.; **Grill:** 12 min.

2 large limes

2 cups liquid margarita mix

1 cup vegetable oil

1 cup chopped fresh cilantro

2 tsp. salt

½ tsp. ground red pepper

3 Tbsp. tequila (optional)

6 skinned and boned chicken breasts

2 cups uncooked long-grain rice

Mango Salsa

Garnish: fresh cilantro sprig

1. Cut limes in half. Squeeze juice into a shallow dish or large zip-top plastic freezer bag; add squeezed lime halves to juice. Add margarita mix, next 4 ingredients, and, if desired, tequila. Whisk (or seal bag and shake) to blend. Add chicken; cover or seal, and chill at least 2 hours or up to 6 hours. Remove chicken from marinade, discarding marinade. Set chicken aside.

2. Prepare rice according to package directions; keep warm.

3. Preheat grill to 300° to 350° (medium) heat. Coat cold grill grate with cooking spray; place on grill.

4. Grill chicken, covered with grill lid, 6 minutes on each side or until a meat thermometer inserted into thickest part of breast registers 165°. Serve over hot cooked rice. Serve with Mango Salsa, and garnish, if desired. **Makes** 6 servings.

Mango Salsa

Prep: 10 min.

2 mangoes, peeled

2 avocados, peeled

1 red bell pepper

½ red onion

1 Tbsp. chopped fresh cilantro

1 Tbsp. vegetable oil

Juice of 1 large lime (about 1 Tbsp.)

1. Chop mangoes, avocados, red bell pepper, and red onion; place in a medium bowl. Add chopped cilantro, oil, and lime juice. Chill, if desired. **Makes** about 2½ cups.

tips from the **pit master**

Use an oven thermometer on the grill grate where the meat will be to determine exact cooking temperature. Built in thermometers are measuring the temperature at the end of the thermometer and not where the meat is. This difference in temperature could be up to 75°.

Molasses-Balsamic Chicken Kabobs With Green Tomatoes and Plums

Prep: 20 min.; **Soak:** 30 min.; **Grill:** 18 min.

8 (12-inch) wooden or metal skewers

1½ lb. skinned and boned chicken breasts, cut into 1½-inch pieces

4 large plums, quartered

2 medium-size green tomatoes, cut into eighths

2 medium-size red onions, cut into eighths

2 tsp. seasoned salt

2 tsp. pepper

½ cup molasses

¼ cup balsamic vinegar

1. Soak wooden skewers in water 30 minutes.

2. Preheat grill to 350° to 400° (medium-high) heat. Thread chicken and next 3 ingredients alternately onto skewers, leaving ¼ inch between pieces. Sprinkle kabobs with seasoned salt and pepper. Stir together molasses and vinegar.

3. Grill kabobs, covered with grill lid, 12 minutes, turning after 6 minutes. Baste kabobs with half of molasses mixture, and grill 3 minutes. Turn kabobs, baste with remaining half of molasses mixture, and grill 3 more minutes or until done. **Makes** 4 to 6 servings.

tools of the trade

Skewers: These are helpful for grilling small vegetables and chunks of meat. You can use either metal or wooden skewers to thread kabobs, but if using wooden skewers, be sure to soak them in water for at least 30 minutes before threading them so that they won't burn on the grill.

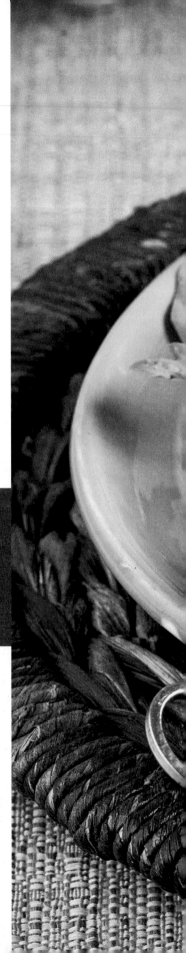

Creole Chicken-and-Sausage Kabobs

Prep: 20 min.; **Soak:** 30 min.; **Grill:** 18 min.

8 (12-inch) wooden or metal skewers

1½ lb. skinned and boned chicken breasts, cut into 1½-inch chunks

¾ lb. smoked sausage, cut into 1-inch slices

½ (16-oz.) package frozen whole okra, thawed

1 large red bell pepper, cut into 1-inch pieces

1½ tsp. Creole seasoning

1. Soak wooden skewers in water 30 minutes.

2. Preheat grill to 350° to 400° (medium-high) heat. Thread chicken, smoked sausage, okra, and bell pepper alternately onto skewers, leaving ¼ inch between pieces; sprinkle with Creole seasoning.

3. Grill kabobs, covered with grill lid, 18 minutes or until a meat thermometer inserted into thickest part of breast registers 165°, turning every 6 minutes. **Makes** 4 to 6 servings.

Grilled Chicken With Orange-Jalapeño Glaze

Prep: 15 min.; **Grill:** 16 min.

Orange-Jalapeño Glaze

10 skinned chicken thighs (about 3 lb.)

½ tsp. salt

½ tsp. pepper

1. Preheat grill to 350° to 400° (medium-high) heat. Prepare, measure, and reserve 1 cup Orange-Jalapeño Glaze.

2. Rinse chicken, and pat dry. Sprinkle evenly with salt and pepper. Brush chicken lightly with remaining ⅔ cup Orange-Jalapeño Glaze.

3. Grill, covered with grill lid, 8 to 10 minutes on each side or until a meat thermometer inserted into thickest portion registers 175°, basting each side with reserved 1 cup glaze during last few minutes. **Makes** 5 servings.

Orange-Jalapeño Glaze

Prep: 15 min.; **Cook:** 15 min.

2 cups orange juice

3 medium jalapeño peppers, seeded and finely chopped

4 garlic cloves, minced

3 Tbsp. orange zest

1 Tbsp. olive oil

3 Tbsp. maple syrup

1 tsp. salt

½ tsp. ground ginger

½ tsp. pepper

1. Stir together all ingredients in a medium saucepan; bring to a boil over medium-high heat. Reduce heat to medium, and cook, stirring often, 15 minutes or until reduced by half. **Makes** 1⅔ cups.

Grilled Herbed Chicken Drumettes With White Barbecue Sauce

Prep: 15 min.; **Chill:** 4 hr.; **Grill:** 20 min.

1 Tbsp. dried thyme

1 Tbsp. dried oregano

1 Tbsp. ground cumin

1 Tbsp. paprika

1 tsp. onion powder

1 tsp. salt

½ tsp. pepper

5 lb. chicken drumettes

Garnish: green onion curls

White Barbecue Sauce

1. Combine first 7 ingredients. Rinse chicken, and pat dry; rub mixture over chicken. Place chicken in a zip-top plastic freezer bag. Seal bag, and chill 4 to 24 hours. Remove chicken from bag, discarding bag.

2. Preheat grill to 350° to 400° (medium-high) heat. Grill chicken, covered with grill lid, 20 to 25 minutes or until done, turning once. Garnish, if desired. Serve with White Barbecue Sauce. **Makes** 12 servings.

White Barbecue Sauce

Prep: 10 min.

1½ cups mayonnaise

¼ cup white wine vinegar

1 garlic clove, minced

1 Tbsp. coarsely ground pepper

1 Tbsp. spicy brown mustard

2 tsp. horseradish

1 tsp. sugar

1 tsp. salt

1. Stir together all ingredients until well blended. Cover and chill until ready to serve. Store in an airtight container in refrigerator up to 1 week. **Makes** 1¾ cups.

'Que and A

Q: I've never heard of white barbecue sauce. What is it and what do I serve it with?

A: White barbecue sauce is a mayonnaise- and vinegar-based sauce believed to hail from north Alabama. It can range in thickness and is typically used with chicken recipes. It's also a great dip for fried onion rings and is tasty drizzled over fried green tomatoes.

W.C. Handy Blues & Barbecue Festival

Henderson, Kentucky

Blues music and barbecue go hand-in-hand at one of the largest free blues music festivals in the country.

What is it?
A week-long free blues music festival with a barbecue competition thrown in.

What is there to do?
• Sit back and enjoy some of the best blues performers from around the country
• Sample barbecue from vendors at "Taste of Henderson Barbecue"

Who hosts it?
The Henderson Music Preservation Society hosts the W.C. Handy Blues and Barbecue Festival each year. All proceeds from the festival are used toward the following year's festival.

How do I get more information?
Visit www.handyblues.org, or call (800) 243-4352.

Photos courtesy of W.C. Handy Blues & Barbecue Festival

Zesty Herb-Citrus Chicken

Heat up the grill, and toss a simple green salad while the chicken marinates for a ready-to-eat meal in less than 40 minutes. Offer fresh fruit as a light and delicious dessert.

Prep: 10 min.; **Chill:** 15 min.; **Grill:** 12 min.

1 (1.06-oz.) package zesty herb marinade

1 tsp. orange zest

¼ cup orange juice

¼ cup vegetable oil

2 lb. skinned and boned chicken breasts or thighs

1. Stir together first 4 ingredients and ¼ cup water in a shallow dish or large zip-top plastic freezer bag. Add chicken, turning to coat. Cover or seal, and chill 15 minutes, turning occasionally. Remove chicken from marinade, discarding marinade.

2. Grill chicken, covered with lid, over medium-high heat (350° to 400°) 6 to 8 minutes on each side or until a meat thermometer inserted into thickest part of breast registers 165° or thigh registers 170°.

Makes 8 servings.

Bacon-Wrapped Barbecue Chicken Kabobs

Chicken and bacon are threaded ribbon-style on these skewers. Serve them with extra barbecue sauce for dipping.

Prep: 15 min.; **Chill:** 1 hr.; **Soak:** 30 min.; **Cool:** 5 min.; **Grill:** 10 min.

⅔ cup barbecue sauce

⅓ cup chili sauce

1½ Tbsp. Worcestershire sauce

12 chicken tenders (about 1½ lb.)

12 wooden skewers

12 bacon slices

1. Whisk together first 3 ingredients in a large shallow dish or zip-top plastic freezer bag; add chicken, turning to coat. Cover or seal, and chill 1 hour, turning once.

2. Meanwhile, soak wooden skewers in water 30 minutes.

3. Preheat grill to 350° to 400° (medium-high) heat. Microwave bacon, in 2 batches, on a microwave-safe plate at HIGH 1 minute. Let cool 5 minutes.

4. Remove chicken from marinade, discarding marinade. Place 1 bacon piece on top of each chicken tender; thread 1 bacon-topped chicken tender onto each skewer.

5. Grill kabobs, covered with grill lid, 5 to 6 minutes on each side or until done. **Makes** 4 to 6 servings.

Molasses-Glazed Chicken Thighs

Skinned and boned chicken thighs are available in the fresh poultry section of most supermarkets.

Prep: 15 min.; **Chill:** 8 hr.; **Grill:** 10 min.

¾ cup molasses

⅓ cup soy sauce

¼ cup fresh lemon juice

¼ cup olive oil

3 garlic cloves, minced

1 tsp. pepper

12 skinned and boned chicken thighs

1. Combine first 6 ingredients in a shallow dish or large zip-top plastic freezer bag; add chicken thighs. Cover or seal, and chill 8 hours, turning occasionally.

2. Preheat grill to 300° to 350° (medium) heat. Remove chicken from marinade, discarding marinade.

3. Grill chicken thighs, covered with grill lid, 5 to 6 minutes on each side or until a thermometer inserted into the thickest part of thighs registers 170°. **Makes** 6 to 8 servings.

Grilled Turkey Drumsticks

Prep: 15 min.; **Chill:** 8 hr.; **Grill:** 1 hr., 20 min.

4 turkey drumsticks

¼ cup butter, melted

⅓ cup vegetable oil

⅓ cup dry sherry

⅓ cup soy sauce

1 garlic clove, minced

¼ cup chopped onion

¼ cup chopped fresh parsley

¼ tsp. salt

¼ tsp. pepper

1. Place drumsticks in a large shallow dish or zip-top plastic freezer bag.

2. Combine butter and next 8 ingredients, stirring well. Pour marinade over drumsticks; cover or seal, and chill 8 hours, turning occasionally. Drain drumsticks, reserving marinade. Wrap each drumstick and ¼ cup marinade in heavy-duty aluminum foil.

4. Preheat grill to 300° to 350° (medium) heat. Grill, covered with grill lid, about 1 hour, turning turkey after 30 minutes. Remove foil, reserving marinade. Return drumsticks to grill, and continue cooking 20 to 30 minutes or until a thermometer inserted into thickest part of drumstick registers 170°, basting frequently with reserved marinade. **Makes** 8 servings.

West Virginia

Here's where to get great 'Q in the state.

Big Frank's Bar-B-Que
211 North 4th Street
Clarksburg
(304) 623-1009

TLP, Inc.
16038 Seneca Trail North
Lewisburg
(304) 497-3011

Cajun-Spiced Catfish Kabobs

A creamy mayonnaise-horseradish sauce works wonderfully with this spicy catfish. Serve with rolls, lettuce, and tomato slices if you want to turn these kabobs into easy po'boys.

Prep: 17 min.; **Chill:** 20 min.; **Cook:** 3 min.; **Grill:** 6 min.

2 tsp. paprika

1 tsp. garlic powder

1 tsp. dried oregano

1 tsp. dried thyme

½ tsp. salt

½ tsp. ground red pepper

4 (6-oz.) catfish fillets, cut into 24 (1-inch) pieces

½ cup mayonnaise

1 Tbsp. fresh lemon juice

2 tsp. capers, chopped

2 tsp. prepared horseradish

2 ears corn, each cut crosswise into 8 pieces

3 green bell peppers, each cut into 8 wedges

8 (12-inch) metal skewers

1. Combine first 6 ingredients in a medium bowl; add catfish, tossing to coat. Cover and refrigerate 20 minutes.

2. Combine mayonnaise, juice, capers, and horseradish in a small bowl; stir with a whisk. Cover and refrigerate.

3. Preheat grill to 350° to 400° (medium-high) heat.

4. Cook the corn in boiling water for 3 minutes, and drain.

5. Thread 3 catfish pieces, 2 corn pieces, and 3 bell pepper pieces alternately onto each of 8 skewers. Place kabobs on a grill rack coated with cooking spray; grill for 3 to 4 minutes on each side or until fish flakes easily with a fork. Serve with sauce. **Makes** 4 servings.

'Que and A

Q: I love the taste of grilled fish, but when I've tried it myself, the fish always sticks or falls apart when I try to take it off the grill. What am I doing wrong?

A: Fish is great on the grill and is a perfect low-calorie dinner option. First, make sure your grill is clean (use a steel-bristle brush) and is very hot. The high heat will create a slight crust on the fish and will allow it to release naturally. If you cook the fish a little longer on the first side, it'll create the crust you're striving for and won't stick when you flip it. Also, try coating your fish with a little oil or cooking spray instead of coating the grates. Make sure you turn the fish only once—fish is more delicate than other meats and can fall apart easily if you mess with it too much. Another option is to use a grill basket—just make sure to remove your fish immediately from the basket once cooked. Otherwise, it may stick.

Fresh Catch Menu

Serves 6 hungry folks

LIME-ORANGE CATFISH

Sweet-and-Spicy Slaw, page 160

Favorite hushpuppies

FRESH-SQUEEZED LEMONADE, PAGE 206

Lime-Orange Catfish

Prep: 15 min.; **Chill:** 15 min.; **Grill:** 10 min.

¼ cup fresh lime juice

⅓ cup orange juice

2 tsp. sugar

1 garlic clove, minced

¼ tsp. salt

½ tsp. dry mustard

½ tsp. paprika

¼ tsp. pepper

2 Tbsp. olive oil

6 (4-oz.) catfish fillets

Garnishes: flat-leaf parsley, orange slices

1. Whisk together first 8 ingredients; gradually whisk in olive oil until well blended. Remove half of juice mixture, and set aside.

2. Place catfish in a shallow dish or zip-top plastic freezer bag; pour remaining marinade over catfish. Cover or seal bag, and chill 15 minutes, turning catfish once.

3. Remove catfish from marinade, discarding marinade.

4. Preheat grill to 350° to 400° (medium-high) heat. Coat grill rack with cooking spray; place on grill. Place catfish on rack, and grill 5 minutes on each side or until done. Remove to a serving platter; drizzle with reserved marinade. Garnish, if desired. **Makes** 6 servings.

Shredded Grilled Tilapia Tacos

Prep: 10 min.; **Grill:** 6 min.

1 Tbsp. ground chipotle seasoning

1½ tsp. ground cumin

½ tsp. salt

6 (6-oz.) tilapia fillets

2 Tbsp. olive oil

1 tsp. lime zest

2 Tbsp. fresh lime juice

12 corn tortillas

Sweet-and-Spicy Slaw

Fruity Black Bean Salsa

Fresh lime wedges

1. Preheat grill to 350° to 400° (medium-high) heat. Combine first 3 ingredients. Gently rub seasoning mixture evenly over fillets.
2. Stir together oil, zest, and juice; rub over fillets.
3. Arrange fillets in a grill basket coated with cooking spray.
4. Grill, without grill lid, 3 minutes on each side or just until fish begins to flake with a fork. Cool slightly. Shred fish. Spoon 2 to 3 Tbsp. fish into tortillas, and top with Sweet-and-Spicy Slaw and Fruity Black Bean Salsa. Serve with a squeeze of fresh lime juice. **Makes** 6 servings.

Sweet-and-Spicy Slaw

Prep: 8 min.

1 cup sour cream

2 Tbsp. rice wine vinegar

2 Tbsp. pineapple or orange marmalade

½ tsp. salt

¼ to ½ tsp. dried chipotle seasoning

1 (16-oz.) package cabbage slaw mix

1. Whisk together first 5 ingredients in a medium glass bowl until blended. Add slaw mix, tossing to coat. Cover and chill until ready to serve. **Makes** 6 servings.

Fruity Black Bean Salsa

Prep: 15 min.

1 (15-oz.) can black beans, rinsed and drained

1 small papaya, peeled, seeded, and cut into ½-inch cubes

½ red or green bell pepper, seeded and chopped

1 large ripe avocado, cut into ½-inch cubes

2 jalapeño peppers, seeded and minced

¼ cup chopped fresh cilantro

1 tsp. lemon zest

2 Tbsp. fresh lemon juice

1 Tbsp. honey

½ tsp. salt

Shopping tip: ½ (24-oz.) jar papaya available in the produce section of your supermarket may be substituted for fresh papaya. If you can't find papaya, substitute 2 ripe mangoes, cubed.

1. Combine black beans and next 5 ingredients in a glass bowl. Whisk together zest and remaining ingredients in a small bowl, and drizzle over bean mixture. Toss gently to coat. Cover and chill salsa until ready to serve. **Makes** 6 servings.

Cedar-Planked Salmon With Barbecue Spice Rub

An assertive spice blend gives salmon a robust taste that works well on its own or to top a salad. Look for cedar planks in gourmet markets or large supermarkets. Alternatively, purchase untreated cedar shingles from lumberyards or hardware stores, and have them cut to the specified size.

Prep: 10 min.; **Soak:** 1 hr., **Grill:** 28 min.

1 (15 x 6½ x ⅜-inch) cedar grilling plank

1½ tsp. kosher salt

1½ tsp. dark brown sugar

1 tsp. ground cumin

1 tsp. dried thyme, crushed

¾ tsp. coarsely ground black pepper

¾ tsp. Hungarian sweet paprika

¾ tsp. chili powder

¼ tsp. ground cinnamon

1 (3-lb.) center-cut salmon fillet, skinned

1. Immerse and soak plank in water 1 hour; drain.
2. Preheat grill to 350° to 400° (medium-high) heat.
3. Combine salt and next 7 ingredients; rub salt mixture over fish.
4. Place plank on grill rack; grill 3 minutes or until lightly charred. Carefully turn plank over; place fish on charred side of plank. Grill, covered with grill lid, 25 minutes or until fish flakes easily when tested with a fork or until desired degree of doneness. Cut fish crosswise into slices. **Makes** 8 to 10 servings.

tools of the trade

Butane Lighter: Forget about matches—butane lighters are easy to use and easy to find. Your hands don't have to get as close to the coals as they would with a match. Even if you have a self-starting gas grill, a butane lighter works nicely as a backup in case it's raining and the self-starter decides to quit on you.

Fresh Herb-Rubbed Salmon Fillets

Prep: 15 min.; **Chill:** 1 hr.; **Cook:** 6 min.

¼ cup tightly packed fresh parsley leaves

¼ cup tightly packed fresh cilantro leaves

¼ cup chopped onion

2 garlic cloves, pressed

3 Tbsp. olive oil

1½ tsp. chili powder

1 tsp. dried oregano

½ tsp. salt

6 (6-oz.) salmon fillets

1. Process first 8 ingredients in a food processor until smooth.
2. Place salmon fillets, skin side down, in a 13- x 9-inch baking dish. Spread herb mixture evenly over fillets; cover and chill 1 hour.
3. Preheat grill to 400° to 500° (high) heat. Grill, skin side down, covered with grill lid, 6 to 10 minutes or until fish flakes with a fork.
Makes 6 servings.

If there's one thing we Southerners can agree on, we love to barbecue.

Citrus Shrimp Tacos

Prep: 25 min.; **Chill:** 10 min.; **Grill:** 4 min.

2 lb. unpeeled, large raw shrimp

20 (12-inch) metal skewers

2 Tbsp. Southwest seasoning

3 garlic cloves, minced

⅓ cup lime juice

3 Tbsp. lemon juice

16 (8-inch) soft taco-size flour tortillas, warmed

1 head iceberg lettuce, finely shredded

1 head radicchio, finely shredded

Southwest Cream Sauce

Grilled Corn Salsa

Garnish: fresh cilantro leaves

Shopping tip: We tested with Emeril's Southwest Seasoning.

1. Peel shrimp; devein, if desired. Thread shrimp onto skewers.
2. Preheat grill to 350° to 400° (medium-high) heat. Combine Southwest seasoning and garlic in a long shallow dish; add lime juice, lemon juice, and shrimp, turning to coat. Cover and chill 10 minutes. Remove shrimp from marinade, discarding marinade.
3. Grill shrimp, without grill lid, 2 to 3 minutes on each side or just until shrimp turn pink. Remove shrimp from skewers. Serve in warm tortillas with next 4 ingredients. Garnish, if desired. **Makes** 6 to 8 servings.

Southwest Cream Sauce

Prep: 10 min.

1 (16-oz.) container sour cream

1 garlic clove, minced

2 Tbsp. finely chopped red onion

1 tsp. chili powder

½ tsp. ground cumin

½ tsp. ground red pepper

¼ tsp. salt

2 Tbsp. chopped fresh cilantro

2 Tbsp. fresh lime juice

1. Whisk together first 7 ingredients. Whisk in cilantro and lime juice until smooth. Cover and chill until ready to serve. **Makes** about 2 cups.

Grilled Corn Salsa

Prep: 25 min.; **Grill:** 15 min.; **Cool:** 15 min.

3 ears fresh corn, husks removed

1 tsp. salt

½ tsp. pepper

3 medium tomatoes, seeded and chopped

2 jalapeño peppers, seeded and minced

2 (15-oz.) cans black beans, rinsed and drained

¾ cup chopped fresh cilantro

⅓ cup fresh lime juice

2 Tbsp. chopped fresh mint

2 avocados

Tortilla chips (optional)

1. Preheat grill to 350° to 400° (medium-high) heat. Lightly coat corn cobs with cooking spray. Sprinkle with salt and pepper.

2. Grill corn, covered with grill lid, 15 to 20 minutes or until golden brown, turning every 5 minutes. Remove from grill; cool 15 minutes.

3. Hold each grilled cob upright on a cutting board; carefully cut downward, cutting kernels from cob. Discard cobs; place kernels in a large bowl. Gently stir in tomatoes and next 5 ingredients. Cover and chill until ready to serve, if desired.

4. If chilled, let corn mixture stand at room temperature 30 minutes. Peel and chop avocados; toss with corn mixture just before serving. Serve with tortilla chips, if desired. **Makes** about 6 cups.

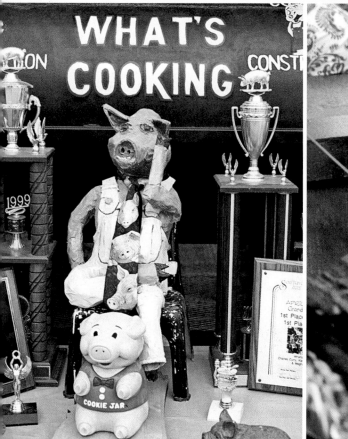

personality
PLUS

Cider Vinegar Barbecue Sauce

Bob Garner, author of *North Carolina Barbecue: Flavored by Time* (John F. Blair, 1996), uses the best of eastern Carolina-style barbecue sauce (vinegar based) and western Carolina-style (tomato based) in this tangy sauce that offers the best of North Carolina barbecue. Use just enough of this sauce to flavor and moisten smoked pork shoulder.

Prep: 10 min.; **Cook:** 7 min.

1½ cups cider vinegar

⅓ cup firmly packed brown sugar

¼ cup ketchup

1 Tbsp. hot sauce

1 tsp. browning and seasoning sauce

½ tsp. salt

½ tsp. onion powder

½ tsp. pepper

½ tsp. Worcestershire sauce

1. Stir together all ingredients in a medium saucepan; cook over medium heat, stirring constantly, 7 minutes or until sugar dissolves. Cover and chill sauce until ready to serve. **Makes** 2 cups.

Sweet Mustard Barbecue Sauce

South Carolinians prefer a mustard-based barbecue sauce. This version is thick and on the tangy-sweet side.

Prep: 8 min.; **Cook:** 10 min.

1 cup cider vinegar

⅔ cup prepared mustard

½ cup sugar

2 Tbsp. chili powder

1 tsp. white peper

1 tsp. black pepper

¼ tsp. ground red pepper

½ tsp. hot sauce

2 Tbsp. butter

½ tsp. soy sauce

1. Stir together first 8 ingredients in a saucepan over medium heat; bring to a boil, reduce heat, and simmer 10 minutes.
2. Remove from heat, and stir in butter and soy sauce. **Makes** about 2 cups.

tools of the trade

Basting brush: Use a basting brush to slather thick sauces onto meats. Most tools labeled "barbecue brushes" are for small jobs. For heftier meats, look for a large paintbrush with natural bristles; synthetic bristles can melt if they touch a hot grate. For easy storage between uses, wash your brushes with hot, soapy water, shake dry, and place in a cup filled with coarse salt. The salt will draw out extra moisture and keep your brushes like new. Just shake off the salt when you're ready to use your brush again.

Tangy White Barbecue Sauce

Prep: 5 min.

1½ cup mayonnaise

⅓ cup apple cider vinegar

¼ cup lemon juice

2 Tbsp. sugar

2 Tbsp. cracked pepper

2 Tbsp. white wine Worcestershire sauce

1. Whisk together all ingredients in a small bowl. Cover and chill until ready to serve. **Makes** about 2¼ cups.

'Que and A

Q: Where did white barbecue sauce originate?

A: "It's the only barbecue sauce we know up here in North Alabama because it's what everybody grows up with," says world barbecue champion Chris Lilly of Big Bob Gibson Bar-B-Q in Decatur, Alabama. Bob Gibson is credited with concocting white sauce in 1925. Like its tomato- and mustard-based cousins, white barbecue sauce comes in shades ranging from porcelain to putty. As for the ingredients, purists such as Myra Grissom, owner of Miss Myra's Pit Bar-B-Q in Birmingham, insists there are only four ingredients: mayonnaise, vinegar, salt, and coarsely ground pepper.

Chipotle Barbecue Sauce

Our Food staff liked this sauce prepared with root beer, but you can substitute cola soft drink too.

Prep: 15 min.; **Cook:** 25 min.

---

1 (10¾-oz.) can tomato puree

1½ cups root beer

1 medium-size sweet onion, finely chopped

¼ cup firmly packed light brown sugar

2 Tbsp. fresh lemon juice

1 tsp. ground chipotle chile powder

1 tsp. salt

¼ tsp. ground cumin

¼ tsp. dried oregano

⅛ tsp. dried crushed red pepper

1. Stir together all ingredients in a 2-qt. saucepan over medium heat. Bring to a boil, stirring frequently. Cover, reduce heat to low, and simmer 25 to 30 minutes or until sauce thickens. **Makes** 3½ cups.

Tangy Honey-Barbecue Sauce

Prep: 10 min.; **Cook:** 15 min.

2 cups ketchup

1 cup dry white wine

⅓ cup honey

1 small onion, diced

2 garlic cloves, minced

1 Tbsp. dried parsley flakes

2 Tbsp. white vinegar

2 Tbsp. lemon juice

1 Tbsp. Worcestershire sauce

1 tsp. hot sauce

¼ tsp. salt

1. Bring all ingredients to a boil in a large saucepan; reduce heat, and simmer, stirring often, 15 to 20 minutes or until slightly thickened. **Makes** about 2¾ cups.

Storage tip: Cover and store leftover sauce in the refrigerator up to 1 week.

Ranch Barbecue Sauce

Prep: 5 min.; **Cook:** 20 min.

1 (18-oz.) bottle barbecue sauce

1 (1-oz.) envelope Ranch dressing mix

¼ cup honey

½ tsp. dry mustard

Shopping tip: We tested with Stubb's Original Bar-B-Q Sauce.

1. Stir together all ingredients in a saucepan over medium-high heat; bring to a boil. Reduce heat, and simmer, stirring occasionally, 20 minutes. **Makes** about 1¼ cups.

'Que and A

Q: Every time I barbecue chicken, the sauce burns. What am I doing wrong?

A: Try basting with the barbecue sauce later in the process, 10 to 15 minutes before the chicken is done. Sauces with a good bit of sugar in them tend to burn if cooked too long.

Spicy Peach Ketchup

Prep: 10 min.; **Chill:** 2 hr.

1 cup ketchup

½ cup thick-and-spicy barbecue sauce

½ cup peach preserves

1. Stir together ketchup, barbecue sauce, and peach preserves until blended. Cover and chill 2 hours. **Makes** 2 cups.

Curry-Apricot Barbecue Sauce

Prep: 5 min.

1 cup barbecue sauce

3 Tbsp. apricot preserves

1 Tbsp. fresh lime juice

1 tsp. curry powder

Shopping tip: We tested with Stubb's Original Bar-B-Q Sauce.

1. Stir together all ingredients in a small bowl. Store in an airtight container in refrigerator up to 5 days. **Makes** about 1⅓ cups.

Tex-Mex Secret Sauce

Prep: 5 min.

½ cup sour cream

⅓ cup ketchup

1 (4.5-oz.) can chopped green chiles

1 Tbsp. minced fresh cilantro

1. Stir together all ingredients. Cover and chill until ready to serve. **Makes** 1 cup.

tips for a tailgate

Mini-sandwiches, called sliders, are all the rage. Pack some small dinner rolls or slider buns for your tailgate, and serve up some pulled pork barbecue, your favorite sauce, and a bowl full of slaw for friends to build their own barbecue sliders. Because pork butt takes a while to cook, you can grill it ahead and store it in the refrigerator for up to two days. Just remember that it's easiest to shred meat while it's warm, so shred it before chilling it or reheat it in the microwave first. Take the hot barbecue in a large insulated container, or reheat it on-site in a slow cooker.

Green Barbecue Sauce

Serve over grilled chicken, fish, or shrimp.

Prep: 15 min.; **Cook:** 2 hr.

2½ lb. green tomatoes, coarsely chopped

1½ lb. tomatillos, husked and coarsely chopped

2 garlic cloves, pressed

½ to 1 cup sugar

1 cup white vinegar

1 large sweet onion, coarsely chopped (about 1½ cups)

1 Tbsp. dry mustard

½ tsp. dried crushed red pepper

1 tsp. salt

1. Cook all ingredients in a large stockpot over medium-low heat 2 hours or until tomatoes and tomatillos are tender. Cool.

2. Process green tomato mixture, in batches, in a food processor or blender until smooth. **Makes** 8 cups.

Storage tip: Sauce may be stored in refrigerator up to 1 week.

Cilantro-Lime Barbecue Sauce

Prep: 5 min.

---

1 cup barbecue sauce

2 Tbsp. chopped fresh cilantro

1 tsp. lime zest

1 Tbsp. fresh lime juice

Shopping tip: We tested with Bull's-Eye Original Barbecue Sauce.

1. Stir together all ingredients in a small bowl. Store in an airtight container in refrigerator up to 5 days. **Makes** about 1 cup.

S. Carolina

Here's where to get great 'Q in the state.

Aiken Brewing Company
140 Laurens Street SW.
Aiken
(803) 502-0707
www.aikenbrewingcompany.com

Jackie Hite's Barbecue
467 West Church Street
Batesburg-Leesville
(803) 532-3354

Shealy's Bar-B-Que
340 East Columbia Avenue
Batesburg-Leesville
(803) 532-8135
www.shealysbbq.com

Bessinger's Bar-Be-Que
1602 Savannah Highway
Charleston
(843) 556-1354
www.bessingersbbq.com

Big T Bar-B-Que
7535-C Garners Ferry Road
Columbia
(803) 776-7132

The Pink Pig
3508 South Okatie Highway
Hardeeville
(843) 784-3635
www.the-pink-pig.com

JOE BESSINGER SR

RESTAURANT BAR-B-Q

BIG T BBQ
and Big T House
WOOD SMOKED SOUTHERN BARBEQUE

HOME
BUFFET
CATERING
BBQ SAUCE

SPECIALS
DIRECTIONS
CONTACT US
T AND S FARM

Shealy's
BAR-B-QUE
40th Anniversary

Chimichurri

This thick, vinegary herb sauce is Argentina's equivalent of the South's barbecue sauce for accompanying smoked or grilled meat or chicken. The sauce's bright green color will darken if you make it ahead, but it tastes just as good.

Prep: 10 min.; **Cook:** 45 sec.; **Stand:** 5 min.

1 Tbsp. dried crushed red pepper

3 Tbsp. red wine vinegar

2 large bunches fresh cilantro, coarsely chopped (about 3 cups)

¼ cup vegetable oil

2 tsp. dried oregano

¼ tsp. ground black pepper

¼ tsp. salt

1. Microwave ¼ cup water at HIGH for 45 seconds. Add crushed red pepper, and let stand 5 minutes. Pour through a fine wire-mesh strainer into a bowl, discarding liquid.

2. Process vinegar, next 5 ingredients, and 2 Tbsp. water in a food processor 5 to 10 seconds or until cilantro is finely chopped. Stir in crushed red pepper. Store in an airtight container up to 3 days. **Makes** ¾ cup.

Melvyn's Seasoning Mix

Ribs seasoned with this Creole-inspired rub are the frequently requested specialty of Melvyn McCoy, owner of Melvyn's restaurant in Monroe, Louisiana. Pair your favorite barbecue sauce with the ribs for serving on the side.

Prep: 5 min.

⅓ cup Creole seasoning

⅓ cup garlic powder

⅓ cup pepper

1½ Tbsp. Greek seasoning

1. Stir together all ingredients. Store in an airtight container. **Makes** about 1¼ cups.

Shopping tip: We tested with Tony Chachere's Original Creole Seasoning and Cavender's All Purpose Greek Seasoning.

If you can't smell it a mile away, it's not worth going.

Dried herbs and spices lose their freshness quickly; use seasonings purchased in the last 6 or 8 months for tastiest results.

Greek Garlic Rub

Prep: 5 min.

1 cup Greek seasoning

¼ cup garlic powder

¼ cup paprika

3 Tbsp. dried oregano

Shopping tip: We tested with Cavender's All Purpose Greek Seasoning.

1. Combine all ingredients. Store in an airtight container. Use to coat lamb, chicken, or beef. **Makes** about 1⅔ cups.

Biltmore Dry Rub

This specialty of Chef Stephen Adams is scaled down in size for home barbecuers. Chef Adams especially likes the rub on lamb.

Prep: 10 min.

¼ cup salt

½ tsp. onion powder

½ tsp. ground celery seeds

½ tsp. garlic powder

½ tsp. paprika

½ tsp. pepper

¼ tsp. dried rosemary

¼ tsp. ground sage

¼ tsp. dried dillweed

1. Combine ingredients. Store in an airtight container up to 6 months. Use to season lamb, chicken, steak, or pork. **Makes** about ¼ cup.

Mediterranean Rub

Prep: 5 min.

2 tsp. ground sage

2 tsp. dried thyme

2 tsp. pepper

1 tsp. salt

1 tsp. garlic powder

1 tsp. dried rosemary, crushed

1. Combine all ingredients. Store in an airtight container. Use to coat lamb, chicken, or beef. **Makes** ¼ cup.

Jamaican Jerk Rub

Prep: 5 min.

⅓ cup freeze-dried chives

1 Tbsp. fine-grain sea salt

1 Tbsp. onion powder

1 Tbsp. dried onion flakes

1 Tbsp. garlic powder

1 Tbsp. ground ginger

1 Tbsp. dried thyme

1 Tbsp. light brown sugar

1 Tbsp. ground red pepper

2 tsp. ground allspice

2 tsp. coarsely ground black pepper

2 tsp. ground coriander

1 tsp. ground cinnamon

½ tsp. ground nutmeg

½ tsp. ground cloves

1. Process all ingredients in a blender until ground and well blended. **Makes** about ¾ cup.

'Que and A

Q: I'd really like to try a rub on some meats. How long do I need to keep the rub on before I start to grill?

A: Rubs are typically a mixture of salt, spices, and herbs and are a great way to add flavor to any type of meat, fish, or vegetable. However, each food to be rubbed has an ideal "sitting" time. For smaller foods like shellfish, kabobs, and vegetables, go up to 15 minutes. For thin fish fillets, lean cuts of meat, chops, and steaks, go up to 30 minutes. For thick cuts of meat, whole chickens, roasts, and bone-in meats, go up to an 1 hour and a half. For large cuts of meat and whole turkeys, go anywhere from 2 to 8 hours.

Southwestern Marinade

Prep: 10 min.

1 small onion, diced

3 garlic cloves, minced

½ cup olive oil

¼ cup lime juice or white wine vinegar

2 Tbsp. Worcestershire sauce

2 tsp. sugar

1 tsp. salt

1 tsp. pepper

1 Tbsp. chopped fresh cilantro

1 tsp. ground cumin

1. Whisk together all ingredients. **Makes** 1¼ cups.

Fresh Herb Marinade

Prep: 10 min.

¼ cup vegetable oil

2 Tbsp. balsamic vinegar

1½ Tbsp. chopped fresh cilantro

1 Tbsp. chopped fresh rosemary

½ tsp. kosher salt

Freshly ground pepper to taste

1. Stir together first 5 ingredients in a small bowl. Season with pepper to taste. **Makes** about ⅓ cup.

Zesty Chicken Marinade

Prep: 10 min.

4 garlic cloves, minced

1 small onion, finely chopped

⅓ cup chopped fresh cilantro

¼ cup olive oil

1½ tsp. paprika

1 tsp. ground cumin

1 tsp. dried parsley

½ tsp. salt

½ tsp. ground red pepper

1. Whisk together all ingredients. **Makes** about ½ cup.

tips for a tailgate

Five tips for stress-free tailgating:
1. Plan your menu ahead of time.
2. Do as much prep work as possible a few days before the game.
3. Store tailgating food in disposable containers.
4. Keep your menu simple.
5. Ask friends to bring their favorite dish or help with the prep work.

Go ahead…give your favorite rib joint some competition.

Tangy-Sweet Soy Marinade

Be sure to whisk the marinade well so that the oil distributes evenly.

Prep: 10 min.

---

1 cup lite soy sauce

6 Tbsp. fresh lime juice
(about 4 limes)

½ cup olive oil

¼ cup water

¼ cup honey

2 garlic cloves, pressed

4 tsp. minced fresh ginger

½ tsp. dried crushed red
pepper

1. Whisk together all ingredients. **Makes** about 2½ cups.

Citrus Marinade

Prep: 5 min.

¾ cup fresh orange juice

2 Tbsp. chopped fresh basil

2 Tbsp. lime juice

2 Tbsp. extra virgin olive oil

½ tsp. dried crushed red
pepper

¼ tsp. salt

1 garlic clove, crushed

1. Whisk together all ingredients. **Makes** 1 cup.

N. Carolina

Here's where to get great 'Q in the state.

12 Bones Smokehouse
5 Riverside Drive
Asheville
(828) 253-4499
www.12bones.com

SKYLIGHT INN
4618 South Lee Street
Ayden
(252) 746-4113

Allen & Son Pit-Cooked Bar-B-Q
6203 Millhouse Road
Chapel Hill
(919) 942-7576

WILBER'S BARBECUE
4172 U.S. 70 East
Goldsboro
(919) 778-5218

Stamey's
2206 High Point Road
Greensboro
(336) 299-9888
www.stameys.com

BAR-B-Q CENTER
900 North Main Street
Lexington
(336) 248-4633
www.barbecuecenter.com

Jimmy's BBQ
1703 Cotton Grove Road
Lexington
(336) 357-2311

LEXINGTON BARBECUE
10 U.S. 29-70 South
Lexington
(336) 249-9814

Speedy's Barbecue
1317 Winston Road
Lexington
(336) 248-2410
www.speedysbbqinc.com

BILLS BARBECUE & CHICKEN
3007 Downing Street SW.
Wilson
(252) 237-4372

Herbed Lemon Marinade and Barbecue Sauce

Prep: 10 min.; **Chill:** 8 hr.

1½ cups lemon juice

2 to 3 garlic cloves, peeled

2 Tbsp. onion powder

1 Tbsp. salt

1 Tbsp. paprika

3 cups vegetable oil

2 Tbsp. dried basil

2 tsp. dried thyme

1. Combine first 5 ingredients in a blender; process on high 1 minute. With blender on high, add oil in a slow, steady stream; process 1 minute. Scrape down sides. Add basil and thyme; process on low 30 seconds. Cover and chill 8 hours or up to 4 days. **Makes** 4½ cups.

Cajun Citrus-Honey Mustard Marinade

Serve grilled chicken made with this marinade with picnic-style side dishes, baked potatoes, and grilled vegetables or your best lettuce or spinach salad.

Prep: 5 min.

⅓ cup honey

¼ cup orange juice

¼ cup olive oil

3 Tbsp. coarse-grained Dijon mustard

2 Tbsp. red wine vinegar

1 Tbsp. Cajun seasoning

2 tsp. hot sauce

1. Whisk together all ingredients. Cover and chill up to 4 days. **Makes** 1 cup.

Black Bean Salsa

Prep: 12 min.; **Chill:** 1 hr.

1 (15-oz.) can black beans, drained

2 canned chipotle chiles in adobo sauce, minced

3 green onions, chopped

½ cup finely chopped yellow bell pepper

1 plum tomato, finely chopped

1 Tbsp. chopped fresh cilantro

2 Tbsp. fresh lime juice

1 Tbsp. olive oil

½ tsp. salt

1. Combine all ingredients in a bowl, tossing well. Cover and chill at least 1 hour. **Makes** about 2¼ cups.

Green Chile Salsa

Prep: 20 min.; **Chill:** 4 hr.

1 (15.5-oz.) can whole tomatoes

3 garlic cloves, chopped

3 jalapeño peppers, seeded and coarsely chopped

2 (4.5-oz.) cans chopped green chiles, drained

6 to 7 green onions, chopped

½ tsp. salt

1. Drain tomatoes, reserving juice in a blender. Add garlic and jalapeño peppers, and process 15 seconds or until smooth, stopping to scrape down sides. Add tomatoes, and pulse 5 times or until coarsely chopped.
2. Stir together tomato mixture, green chiles, green onions, and salt. Cover and chill 4 hours. **Makes** 4 cups.

tips for a tailgate

For a fun and easy entertaining idea, set up a salsa bar. Take your pick of these salsas, transport them in a cooler, and pull them out to nibble on with chips as the main course grills before the game.

Quick-and-Easy Picante Sauce

This superfast salsa has a thick consistency and smooth appearance similar to a picante-style salsa. Canned tomato products will vary in sweetness and salt, so be sure to taste before adding sugar or salt.

Prep: 5 min.; **Chill:** 30 min.

1 (28-oz.) can diced tomatoes

1 (10-oz.) can diced tomatoes with green chiles, drained

½ cup diced sweet onion

½ tsp. garlic powder

½ tsp. ground cumin

½ tsp. freshly ground pepper

2 Tbsp. fresh lime juice

2 Tbsp. chopped fresh cilantro (optional)

1 Tbsp. sugar (optional)

¾ tsp. salt (optional)

1. Stir together first 7 ingredients and, if desired, cilantro, sugar, and salt. Cover and chill 30 minutes. **Makes** 4 cups.

Pineapple Salsa

Prep: 15 min.

¼ cup orange juice

2 Tbsp. lemon juice

1 Tbsp. honey

¼ tsp. salt

¼ tsp. pepper

2 cups chopped fresh pineapple

2 Tbsp. chopped fresh cilantro

¼ small red onion, chopped

1. Whisk together first 5 ingredients. Stir in pineapple, cilantro, and onion. Cover and chill until ready to serve. **Makes** 2 cups.

Blueberry Salsa

This fruity salsa is a refreshing side to grilled meats and fish.

Prep: 15 min.

2 cups chopped fresh blueberries

1 cup whole fresh blueberries

¼ cup fresh lemon juice

3 Tbsp. chopped fresh cilantro

2 seeded and minced jalapeño peppers

⅓ cup diced red bell pepper

¼ cup chopped onion

½ tsp. kosher salt

1. Stir together all ingredients; cover and chill until ready to serve. **Makes** about 3 cups.

International Bar-B-Q Festival

Owensboro, Kentucky

Enjoy a family weekend with a pie-eating contest, carnival rides, and, of course, The Classic Cook-Off barbecue competition.

What is it?

An event for all ages including: The Classic Cook-Off; local, regional, and national entertainers; carnival rides; and pageants.

What is there to do?

• Stop by the pie-eating contest and test your culinary limits

• Enjoy the carnival area set up to please all members of the family

• The 5K Run/Walk will help you work up an appetite so you can pig out on the competition food

• Participate in the horseshoe toss, burgoo relay, or keg toss

Who hosts it?

The Owensboro Daviess Convention and Visitors Bureau hosts the International Bar-B-Q Festival.

How do I get more information?

Visit www.bbqfest.com, or call (800) 489-1131 or (270) 926-6938.

Photos courtesy of OnSite Images

Chili-Lime Butter

Nothing—repeat, nothing—tastes better in the summer than fresh corn on the cob. Just cook up your favorite variety, and then flavor it with this tasty butter.

Prep: 5 min.

½ cup softened butter

2 tsp. lime zest

½ tsp. chili powder

Salt and pepper to taste

1. Stir softened butter; stir in lime zest and remaining ingredients.
Makes ½ cup.

Blue Cheese Butter

Prep: 5 min.; **Chill:** 8 hr.

¼ cup crumbled blue cheese

½ cup butter, softened

1. Stir blue cheese into butter; cover and chill 8 hours. Serve with crackers as an hors d'oeuvre or on baked potatoes or steaks. **Makes** ¾ cup.

Peppy Basil Butter

Our Food staff especially liked this with steamed fresh artichokes.

Prep: 5 min.; **Stand:** 10 min.

⅓ cup butter

3 Tbsp. chopped fresh basil

½ tsp. salt

¼ tsp. dried crushed red pepper

1. Microwave butter in a microwave-safe glass bowl at HIGH 30 to 45 seconds or until melted and hot. Stir in chopped fresh basil, salt, and dried crushed red pepper. Let stand 10 minutes before serving. **Makes** about ⅓ cup.

Spicy Chipotle Mayonnaise

Prep: 10 min.

½ cup mayonnaise

1 Tbsp. chopped chipotle peppers in adobo sauce

¼ tsp. lime zest

1 tsp. fresh lime juice

1. Stir together all ingredients Cover and chill until ready to serve. Store in an airtight container in refrigerator up to 1 week. **Makes** ½ cup.

Tomato-Basil Mayonnaise

Prep: 5 min.

1½ cups mayonnaise

½ cup fresh basil leaves

2 Tbsp. tomato sauce

1. Process mayonnaise, basil leaves, and tomato sauce in a blender or food processor until smooth, stopping to scrape down sides. Store in an airtight container in refrigerator up to 1 week. **Makes** about 1½ cups.

tips for a tailgate

It's easy to smoke a turkey breast a day or two ahead for quick and easy sandwiches on game day. Transport one or both of these flavored mayonnaises in the cooler for jazzing up the turkey on choices of wheat bread, focaccia, or hoagie buns. Set out sliced cheeses, tomatoes, pickles, and red onion as well as leaf lettuce from the cooler for a sandwich smorgasbord.

ALL the fix in's

Spring Menu

Serves 8 hungry folks

CEDAR-PLANKED SALMON WITH BARBECUE SPICE RUB, PAGE 163

Grilled Artichokes and Asparagus, page 257

Rice pilaf or orzo

MINT TEA PUNCH OR STRAWBERRY TEA SLUSH, PAGE 206

Mint Tea Punch

Prep: 10 min.; **Steep:** 10 min.

5 cups boiling water

5 regular-size tea bags

8 mint sprigs, crushed

1 cup sugar

1 (12-oz.) can frozen orange juice concentrate, thawed and undiluted

1 (12-oz.) can frozen lemonade concentrate, thawed and undiluted

Garnishes: fresh mint sprigs, lemon slices

1. Pour 5 cups boiling water over tea bags; add mint sprigs. Cover and steep 5 minutes. Stir in sugar; steep 5 more minutes.

2. Remove tea bags. Pour tea through a fine wire-mesh strainer into a pitcher, discarding mint sprigs. Stir in concentrates and 6¾ cups water. Chill. Serve over ice. Garnish, if desired. **Makes** 14 cups.

Southern Sweet Tea

If you like tea that's really sweet, add the full cup of sugar.

Prep: 5 min.; **Cook:** 5 min.; **Steep:** 10 min.

2 family-size tea bags

½ to 1 cup sugar

7 cups cold water

1. Bring 3 cups water to a boil in a saucepan; add tea bags. Boil 1 minute; remove from heat. Cover and steep 10 minutes.
2. Remove and discard tea bags. Add desired amount of sugar, stirring until dissolved.
3. Pour into a 1-gal. container, and add 7 cups cold water. Serve over ice. **Makes** 10 cups.

Tea 'n' Lemonade

Prep: 5 min.; **Cook:** 5 min.; **Steep:** 10 min.

2 qt. Southern Sweet Tea made with ½ cup sugar

1 cup thawed lemonade concentrate

1. Stir together 2 qt. Southern Sweet Tea made with ½ cup sugar; add thawed lemonade concentrate, and stir well. Serve over ice. **Makes** 9 cups.

tips for a tailgate

Sweet tea and lemonade are popular partners for barbecue and travel well to tailgates and picnics iced down in a cooler. These recipes easily double if needed to refresh a thirsty crowd.

Peach Iced Tea

Prep: 5 min.; **Cook:** 5 min.; **Steep:** 10 min.

1½ qt. Southern Sweet Tea made with ½ cup sugar

1 (33.8-oz.) bottle peach nectar

¼ cup lemon juice

1. Stir together 1½ qt. Southern Sweet Tea made with ½ cup sugar; add peach nectar and lemon juice. Stir well. Serve over ice. **Makes** about 10 cups.

Strawberry Tea Slush

Prep: 15 min.; **Steep:** 5 min.; **Chill:** 1 hr.

2 cups boiling water

4 regular-size tea bags

1½ cups frozen strawberries

1 (6-oz.) can frozen lemonade concentrate

1 cup ice cubes

¼ cup powdered sugar

1. Pour 2 cups boiling water over tea bags. Cover and steep 5 minutes. Remove tea bags. Chill at least 1 hour.

2. Process chilled tea, frozen strawberries, and remaining ingredients in a blender until smooth and slushy. Serve immediately. **Makes** 6 cups.

Fresh-Squeezed Lemonade

Prep: 20 min.

1½ cups sugar

½ cup boiling water

1 Tbsp. lemon zest

1½ cups fresh lemon juice
(8 large lemons)

1. Stir together 1½ cups sugar and ½ cup boiling water until sugar is dissolved. Stir in lemon zest, lemon juice, and 5 cups water. Cover and chill. Serve over ice. **Makes** 8 cups.

Cherry-Berry Lemonade

Prep: 10 min.

1 (16-oz.) package frozen mixed berries, thawed

1 (16-oz.) jar maraschino cherries without stems

1¼ cups sugar

¾ cup fresh lemon juice (about 5 lemons)

¼ cup fresh lime juice (about 1 large lime)

1. Process all ingredients in a blender until smooth, stopping to scrape down sides. Pour fruit mixture through a wire-mesh strainer into a pitcher, discarding solids. Stir in 2 cups water. Serve over ice. **Makes** 5 cups.

Watermelon-Lemonade Cooler

Prep: 25 min.; **Cook:** 10 min.; **Chill:** 8 hr.

15 cups seeded and cubed watermelon

2 (12-oz.) cans frozen lemonade concentrate, thawed

2 mint sprigs

1. Process watermelon, in batches, in a blender or food processor until smooth.

2. Combine concentrate and 2 mint sprigs, and cook in a saucepan over medium-high heat 10 minutes. Stir together watermelon puree and lemonade mixture; cover and chill 8 hours. Remove and discard mint. Stir and serve over ice. **Makes** 14 cups.

tips for a tailgate

This refreshing beverage is the perfect make-ahead thirst-quencher. Whip it up the day before the game, and refrigerate it in a large jar or thermos. Don't forget to pack ice to scoop into plastic cups as well as for nestling canned drinks.

Pineapple-Buttermilk Shake

Prep: 10 min.

1 (8-oz.) can unsweetened pineapple chunks, drained and frozen

1 qt. vanilla ice cream

½ cup firmly packed brown sugar

2 cups buttermilk

1. Process all ingredients in a blender until smooth, stopping to scrape down sides. Serve immediately. **Makes** 6 cups.

Light Pineapple-Buttermilk Shake: Substitute low-fat vanilla ice cream and fat-free buttermilk; reduce brown sugar to ⅓ cup. Proceed with recipe as directed, and serve immediately.

Scarlet Margaritas

If pomegranates are not available, no problem. This drink is just as delicious without the fresh seeds.

Prep: 10 min.

4 cups crushed ice

1 cup pomegranate juice

½ cup orange liqueur

½ cup tequila

1 Tbsp. lime juice

4 Tbsp. pomegranate seeds
(½ fresh pomegranate)
(optional)

Lime wedges

Coarse salt

Garnish: lime slices

Shopping tip: We tested
with Pom Wonderful 100%
Pomegranate Juice.

1. Process first 5 ingredients, and, if desired, pomegranate seeds in a blender 30 seconds or until frothy.
2. Rub rims of 6 glasses with lime wedges; dip in salt to coat. Pour margarita evenly into prepared glasses. Garnish, if desired. Serve immediately.
Makes 6 servings.

Watermelon Daiquiri

Prep: 20 min.; **Freeze:** 8 hr.

4 cups seeded and cubed watermelon

⅓ cup light rum

¼ to ½ cup orange juice

2 Tbsp. orange liqueur

4 tsp. powdered sugar

2 tsp. fresh lime juice

Shopping tip: We tested with Cointreau for orange liqueur.

1. Place watermelon in a zip-top plastic freezer bag. Seal bag; freeze 8 hours.

2. Process watermelon, rum, and remaining ingredients in a blender or food processor until smooth, stopping to scrape down sides. Serve immediately. **Makes** 3 cups.

Tequila Mojitos

The simple syrup needed for this beverage may be made up to one week ahead and stored in the refrigerator.

Prep: 10 min.; **Cook:** 8 min.; **Stand:** 2 hr.

¾ cup sugar

1 cup fresh mint sprigs

2 cups lemon-lime soft drink, chilled

1 cup fresh lime juice

½ cup tequila

Garnishes: fresh mint sprigs, lime slices

1. Bring 1 cup water and sugar to a boil in a medium saucepan. Boil, stirring often, until sugar dissolves. Remove from heat; add mint sprigs, and let stand 2 hours or until mixture is completely cool.

2. Pour mixture through a wire-mesh strainer into a pitcher, discarding mint. Stir in lemon-lime soft drink, lime juice, and tequila. Serve over ice. Garnish, if desired. **Makes** 5 cups.

Magnolia Blossom Festival

Magnolia, Arkansas

The Magnolia Blossom Festival ensures fun for the entire family with its art shows and world championship steak cook-off.

What is it?

An event including the Annual World Championship Steak Cook-off, sidewalk art show, grilling cooking schools, and entertainment for the entire family.

What is there to do?

• Enjoy a steak cook-off competition judging everything from the way grills are decorated to the tenderness of the steak
• Participate in the Blossom Festival Parade or the Magnolia Blossom Pageant
• Stop by the grilling cooking class to enhance your outdoor culinary skills

Who hosts it?

The Magnolia/Columbia County Chamber of Commerce hosts the Magnolia Blossom Festival and World Championship Steak Cook-off.

How do I get more information?

Visit www.blossomfestival.org, or call (870) 234-4352.

Photos courtesy of the Magnolia/Columbia County Chamber of Commerce

Frozen Sangría

This sangría makes about 24 servings without breaking the bank. Total cost is about $13.

Prep: 10 min.; **Freeze:** 24 hr.

1 gal. sangría

1 (12-oz.) can frozen limeade, thawed

1 (2-liter) bottle lemon-lime soft drink

2 cups sliced oranges, lemons, and limes

Shopping tip: Substitute cranberry juice for sangría if you prefer a kid-friendly, nonalcoholic drink.

1. Place 1 (2-gal.) zip-top plastic freezer bag inside another 2-gal. zip-top plastic freezer bag. Place bags in a large bowl. Combine sangría, limeade, and lemon-lime soft drink in the inside bag. Seal both bags, and freeze 24 hours. (Double bagging is a precaution to avoid spills.)

2. Remove mixture from freezer 1 hour before serving, squeezing occasionally until slushy. Transfer mixture to a 2-gal. container. Stir in fruit. **Makes** about 24 cups.

Porter Float

Dark beer gives the ice-cream float a new dimension.

Prep: 2 min.

Vanilla ice cream

3 to 4 Tbsp. creamy porter or stout beer

Fresh raspberries

Fresh mint sprig

Shopping tip: We tested with Samuel Smith Oatmeal Stout.

1. Scoop ice cream into a tall glass, filling two-thirds full. Top with a few tablespoonfuls of beer. Top with raspberries and a mint sprig. **Makes** 1 serving.

Sweet-'n'-Salty Honey Cheese Spread

Prep: 10 min.

1 (10.5-oz.) goat cheese log

½ cup roasted, salted sunflower seeds

⅓ cup honey

1 pt. fresh raspberries, blackberries, or blueberries

Assorted crackers

1. Press or roll goat cheese log in sunflower seeds, thoroughly covering cheese, including ends. Arrange cheese on a serving platter with any remaining sunflower seeds. Drizzle with honey. Sprinkle with berries. Serve immediately with assorted crackers. **Makes** 10 appetizer servings.

Dixie Caviar

Prep: 15 min.; **Chill:** 24 hr.

2 (15.8-oz.) cans black-eyed peas, rinsed and drained

2 cups frozen whole kernel corn

2 medium tomatoes, finely chopped

1 medium-size green bell pepper, finely chopped

1 small sweet onion, finely chopped

4 green onions, sliced

1 to 2 jalapeño peppers, seeded and minced

1 to 2 garlic cloves, minced

1 cup Italian dressing

¼ cup chopped fresh cilantro

½ cup sour cream

Tortilla chips

1. Combine first 9 ingredients in a large zip-top plastic freezer bag. Seal and chill 24 hours; drain.

2. Spoon mixture into a serving bowl. Stir in cilantro, and top with sour cream. Serve with tortilla chips. **Makes** 6 cups.

Barbecue Ranch Dip

Prep: 5 min.; **Chill:** 30 min.

1 (1-oz.) envelope Ranch dressing mix

1½ cups light sour cream

2 Tbsp. barbecue sauce

Roasted new potatoes

1. Whisk together first 3 ingredients. Cover and chill 30 minutes. Serve with roasted red new potatoes. **Makes** about 1½ cups.

Tennessee

Here's where to get great 'Q in the state.

Rib & Loin Bar-B-Q

5946 Brainerd Road
Chattanooga
(423) 499-6465
www.ribandloin.com

Shuford's Smokehouse

924 Signal Mountain Road
Chattanooga
(423) 267-0080
www.shufordsbbq.com

Buddy's Bar-B-Q

5806 Kingston Pike
Knoxville
(865) 588-0051
www.buddysbarbq.com

Bar-B-Q Shop

1782 Madison Avenue
Memphis
(901) 272-1277

Charlie Vergos Rendezvous

52 South Second Street
Memphis
(901) 523-2746
www.hogsfly.com

Corky's Ribs & BBQ

5259 Poplar Avenue
Memphis
(901) 685-9744
corkysribsandbbq.com

Jim Neely's Interstate Bar-B-Que

2265 South Third Street
Memphis
(901) 775-2304
www.interstatebarbecue.com

Neely's Bar-B-Que

670 Jefferson Avenue
Memphis
(901) 521-9798
www.neelysbbq.com

Barbecue Bean Dip

To make ahead, stir together bean mixture the day before; cover and chill. Let sit at room temperature 30 minutes before baking.

Prep: 15 min.; **Cook:** 25 min.

4 slices bacon, cooked and crumbled

1 small sweet onion, chopped

1 (14.5-oz.) can great Northern beans, rinsed and drained

¼ cup spicy barbecue sauce

¼ cup tomato sauce

¼ tsp. garlic powder

½ cup (2 oz.) shredded Cheddar cheese

Corn chip scoops

1. Preheat oven to 350°. Process bacon and next 5 ingredients in a food processor until smooth, stopping to scrape down sides.
2. Spread bacon mixture into a 1-qt. baking dish or a 9-inch pie plate.
3. Bake at 350° for 20 minutes; sprinkle cheese evenly over top, and bake 5 more minutes. Serve immediately with chips. **Makes** 8 servings.

Grilled Pizza With Steak, Pear, and Arugula

Prep: 10 min.; **Grill:** 25 min.; **Stand:** 10 min.

½ pound flank steak

Salt and pepper

1 Tbsp. olive oil

1½ tsp. white balsamic vinegar

1 (12-inch) prebaked pizza crust

1 red Bartlett pear, peeled and sliced

1½ cups fresh arugula, divided

¼ cup crumbled Gorgonzola cheese

Freshly cracked pepper

Shopping tip: We tested with ½ (16-oz.) package Mama Mary's Thin & Crispy Pizza Crusts.

1. Coat cold cooking grate of grill with cooking spray, and place on grill. Preheat grill to 300° to 350° (medium) heat.
2. Season flank steak with salt and pepper.
3. Grill steak, covered with grill lid, 8 to 10 minutes on each side or to desired degree of doneness. Cover and let stand 10 minutes.
4. Meanwhile, whisk together oil and vinegar in a small bowl.
5. Cut steak diagonally across grain into thin strips. Cut strips into bite-size pieces (about 1 cup).
6. Place pizza crust directly on hot cooking grate. Brush top of crust with oil mixture; layer with pear slices, 1 cup arugula, cheese, and beef strips.
7. Grill, covered, 4 minutes. Rotate pizza one-quarter turn; grill, covered, 5 to 6 more minutes or until thoroughly heated. Remove pizza from grill, and sprinkle with remaining ½ cup arugula and freshly cracked pepper. **Makes** 4 servings.

Oven-Baked Pizza With Steak, Pear, and Arugula: Assemble pizza as directed, and bake according to package directions for pizza crust.

220

Grilled Pork, Cheddar, and Jalapeño Sausage

This is adapted from a popular sausage at HEB's Central Market in Austin.

Prep: 10 min.; **Cook:** 24 min.

2 lb. mild ground pork sausage

2 cups (8 oz.) shredded sharp Cheddar cheese

1 small onion, chopped

2 large jalapeño peppers, seeded and chopped

5 garlic cloves, minced

1 tsp. salt

1 Tbsp. pepper

1. Beat all ingredients at medium speed with an electric mixer until blended. Shape into 12 patties.

2. Prepare fire by piling charcoal or lava rocks on 1 side of grill, leaving the other side empty. Coat food rack with cooking spray, and place on grill. Arrange patties over empty side; grill, covered with grill lid, over high heat (400° to 500°) 12 minutes on each side or until done. **Makes** 12 patties.

Carolina Grilled Shrimp

Prep: 20 min.; **Soak:** 30 min.; **Chill:** 20 min.; **Grill:** 4 min.

4 (12-inch) wooden skewers

1 lb. unpeeled, jumbo raw shrimp (16/20 count)

2 Tbsp. olive oil

¼ cup chili sauce

2 Tbsp. fresh lemon juice

2 Tbsp. Worcestershire sauce

2 garlic cloves, minced

¼ tsp. ground red pepper

1. Soak wooden skewers in water 30 minutes.

2. Peel shrimp; devein, if desired. Thread shrimp onto skewers. Place in a 13- x 9-inch baking dish.

3. Whisk together olive oil and next 5 ingredients in a bowl; pour over shrimp. Cover and chill 20 minutes. Remove shrimp from marinade, discarding marinade.

4. Preheat grill to 350° to 400° (medium-high) heat. Grill shrimp, covered with grill lid, 2 to 3 minutes on each side or just until shrimp turn pink.

Makes 4 appetizer servings.

his refreshing appetizer, inspired by a recipe from chef Robert
St. John's book *A Southern Palate,* showcases Gulf Coast shrimp.

Prep: 15 min.; **Chill:** 8 hr.

cup olive oil

cup white balsamic vinegar

Tbsp. chopped fresh cilantro

Tbsp. lemon zest

sp. salt

sp. freshly ground pepper

sp. hot sauce

lb. peeled, large cooked
shrimp

Romaine lettuce heart leaves

1. Whisk together olive oil, balsamic vinegar, and next 5 ingredients in a large bowl.

2. Place cooked shrimp and vinaigrette mixture in a large zip-top plastic freezer bag. Seal and chill at least 8 hours or up to 24 hours, turning bag occasionally.

3. Arrange lettuce leaves in 8 (6- to 8-oz.) glasses. Spoon shrimp mixture evenly into glasses. **Makes** 8 servings.

Make-ahead tip: Vinaigrette may be prepared ahead and stored in an airtight container in the refrigerator up to 1 week. Let vinaigrette come to room temperature, and whisk before adding cooked shrimp.

Lemon Scallops on Rosemary Skewers

For easier turning on the grill and added rosemary flavor, use two rosemary sprigs as each skewer.

Prep: 15 min.; **Chill:** 30 min.; **Soak:** 20 min.; **Grill:** 4 min.

12 large sea scallops

1 Tbsp. olive oil

2 teaspoons lemon juice

1 tsp. finely chopped fresh rosemary

¼ tsp. Kosher salt

⅛ tsp. freshly ground pepper

8 (12-inch) fresh rosemary sprigs

Garnish: lemon slices

1. Combine first 6 ingredients in a medium bowl; cover and chill 30 minutes.
2. Preheat grill to 350° to 400° (medium-high) heat.
3. Pick leaves off 6 inches of 1 end of each rosemary sprig, leaving the other end intact. Soak rosemary sprigs in water in a shallow dish 20 minutes.
4. Place 2 rosemary skewers side by side, leaving a small space between. Thread 3 scallops onto bare part of rosemary skewers. Repeat with remaining rosemary and scallops. Grill, uncovered, 2 to 3 minutes on each side. Garnish with lemon slices, if desired. **Makes** 4 servings.

tips for a tailgate

Kabobs are a great make-ahead dish for your tailgate. You can assemble them at home, chill them in a cooler, and throw them on the grill while gearing up for the big game.

Grilled Scallops With Creole Tomato Sauce

Prep: 12 min.; **Grill:** 4 min.

24 large sea scallops
(about 2¼ lb.)

2 Tbsp. olive oil

¾ tsp. kosher salt

½ tsp. freshly ground pepper

Creole Tomato Sauce

Garnish: fresh thyme sprigs

1. Preheat grill to 400° to 500° (high) heat. Brush scallops with olive oil; sprinkle with salt and pepper.
2. Grill, uncovered, 4 to 5 minutes or just until scallops are opaque, turning once. Serve warm with Creole Tomato Sauce. Garnish, if desired. **Makes** 8 appetizer servings.

Creole Tomato Sauce

Prep: 12 min.; **Cook:** 10 min.

¾ cup finely chopped onion

¾ cup finely chopped red bell pepper

1 Tbsp. minced garlic

1 tsp. dried thyme

½ tsp. dried oregano

⅛ tsp. ground red pepper

1 Tbsp. olive oil

⅓ cup dry white wine

1 (14½-oz.) can diced tomatoes, undrained

¼ tsp. kosher salt

¼ tsp. freshly ground black pepper

1. Sauté onion and next 5 ingredients in hot oil in a large skillet over medium-high heat about 5 minutes or until vegetables are tender. Add wine, and cook until most of the liquid evaporates. Stir in tomatoes, salt, and pepper; cook 5 to 7 minutes or until mixture thickens, stirring occasionally. Cool slightly. Process tomato mixture in a blender or food processor until smooth. Return sauce to skillet; keep warm.
Makes 1¾ cups.

Mini Cajun Burgers With Easy Rémoulade

Prep: 20 min.; **Grill:** 10 min.

1¼ lb. ground beef

½ pound spicy Cajun sausage, finely chopped

2 tsp. Cajun seasoning

1 (14-oz.) package dinner rolls, split

Green leaf lettuce

Easy Rémoulade

1. Combine ground beef and sausage in a large bowl. Shape mixture into 12 (2½-inch) patties, and place on a large baking sheet. Sprinkle patties evenly with Cajun seasoning. Cover and chill up to 1 day, if desired.
2. Preheat grill to 350° to 400° (medium-high) heat. Grill, covered, 5 minutes on each side or until no longer pink in center. Serve on split rolls with green leaf lettuce and Easy Rémoulade. **Makes** 12 appetizer servings.

Easy Rémoulade

Prep: 5 min.; **Chill:** 30 min.

¾ cup light mayonnaise

2 Tbsp. Creole mustard

2 Tbsp. chopped fresh parsley

1. Combine all ingredients. Cover and chill 30 minutes or up to 3 days. **Makes** 1 cup.

tips for a tailgate

Prepare patties the night before the game. Stack between sheets of wax paper, place in a disposable plastic container, cover with lid, and refrigerate overnight. Transport patties safely by packing in a cooler with ice. They'll be ready for the grill once you arrive at your destination.

Bacon-and-Chicken Bites in Sweet-Hot Mustard

The sweet and spicy kick in this Asian-inspired marinade gets its flavor from orange marmalade, soy sauce, and ginger. For dinner, serve the chicken atop a bed of rice or with a side green salad.

Prep: 10 min.; **Chill:** 2 hr.; **Grill:** 8 min.

---

2 (8-oz.) boneless, skinless chicken breasts

8 bacon slices, cut into thirds

½ cup orange marmalade

¼ cup lite soy sauce

3 Tbsp. Dijon mustard

¾ tsp. ground ginger

¼ tsp. garlic powder

Shopping tip: We tested with Pilgrim's Pride Boneless, Skinless Chicken Breasts.

1. Cut chicken breasts into 24 (1-inch) pieces. Wrap each chicken piece with 1 piece of bacon, and secure with a wooden pick.

2. Stir together orange marmalade and next 4 ingredients in a large bowl; remove and reserve ¼ cup mixture. Add chicken to bowl, tossing to coat. Cover and chill 2 hours, turning occasionally. Remove chicken from marinade, discarding marinade.

3. Preheat grill to 350° to 400° (medium-high) heat. Grill chicken, covered with grill lid, 4 to 5 minutes on each side or until done. Toss chicken with reserved marinade before serving. **Makes** 6 appetizer servings.

Finishing tip: Once the chicken is grilled and has been tossed with the marinade, sprinkle with some toasted sesame seeds.

tips from the **pit master**

Use a good set of tongs to handle meat on the grill instead of a long fork to prevent piercing the meat, which will allow juices to escape.

Bacon-Wrapped Mushrooms With Honey-Barbecue Sauce

Prep: 15 min.; **Cook:** 3 min.; **Grill:** 8 min.

24 small fresh mushrooms

12 bacon slices

1 cup Honey-Barbecue Sauce

1. Preheat grill to 350° to 400° (medium-high) heat. Wash mushrooms thoroughly. Cut bacon slices in half crosswise, and microwave, in 2 batches, at HIGH 1½ to 2 minutes or until bacon is partially cooked. Pat dry with paper towels. Wrap each mushroom with a bacon slice, and secure with wooden picks. Dip wrapped mushrooms in Honey-Barbecue Sauce.
2. Grill mushrooms (using a grill basket, if necessary), covered with grill lid, 4 to 5 minutes on each side or until bacon is crisp and thoroughly cooked. **Makes** 8 appetizer servings.

Honey-Barbecue Sauce

Prep: 10 min.; **Cook:** 15 min.

2 cups ketchup

1 cup dry white wine

⅓ cup honey

1 small onion, diced

2 garlic cloves, minced

1 Tbsp. dried parsley flakes

2 Tbsp. white vinegar

2 Tbsp. lemon juice

1 Tbsp. Worcestershire sauce

1 tsp. hot sauce

¼ tsp. salt

1. Bring all ingredients to a boil in a large saucepan; reduce heat, and simmer, stirring often, 15 to 20 minutes or until slightly thickened. **Makes** about 2¾ cups.

Storage tip: Cover and store leftover sauce in the refrigerator up to 1 week.

Carolina Mountain Ribfest

Fletcher, North Carolina

Top name entertainers and professional barbecue masters roll into North Carolina for this annual event.

What is it?

An event that is fun for the entire family featuring professional barbecue rib vendors from around the country, top-name entertainment, an arts and crafts show, bike and car shows, and a carnival with spectacular adult and children's rides and games.

What is there to do?

• Sample traditional barbecue from world-class professional rib vendors
• Tap your toes to music from top names in the entertainment world
• Cruise bike and car shows, arts and crafts

Who hosts it?

Western Carolina Productions hosts the Carolina Mountain Ribfest at the WNC Agricultural Center Fairgrounds.

How do I get more information?

Visit www.wcpshows.com, or call (828) 628-9626.

Photos courtesy of Western Carolina Productions, Inc.

Prosciutto-Wrapped Figs Stuffed With Blue Cheese

Crisp prosciutto and tart cheese pair well with the juicy, sweet grilled figs to make a memorable appetizer.

Prep: 22 min.; **Cook:** 10 min.; **Grill:** 6 min.

12 large fresh black Mission figs, trimmed

2 oz. blue cheese, cut into 12 cubes

2 oz. thinly sliced prosciutto, cut into 12 strips

¼ cup balsamic vinegar

2 Tbsp. honey

⅛ tsp. freshly ground black pepper

Dash of salt

1. Cut each fig in half vertically, cutting to, but not through, base of fig. Spread slightly apart. Place 1 cube of cheese inside each fig; gently close to seal. Wrap 1 prosciutto strip around each fig.
2. Preheat grill to 350° to 400° (medium-high) heat.
3. Combine vinegar and next 3 ingredients in a small saucepan; bring to a boil. Reduce heat, and simmer until thick, about 10 minutes. Cool.
4. Place figs on grill rack coated with cooking spray; grill 4 to 6 minutes, turning occasionally, until prosciutto is crisp. Drizzle each fig with balsamic syrup. **Makes** 6 servings.

Open House Menu

Serves 8 to 10 hungry folks

MINI CAJUN BURGERS WITH EASY RÉMOULADE, PAGE 229

Grilled Herbed Chicken Drumettes
With White Barbecue Sauce, page 150

Bacon-Wrapped Mushrooms, page 232, or Proscuitto-Wrapped Figs Stuffed With Blue Cheese, opposite page

GOAT CHEESE WITH MARINATED ROASTED PEPPERS

Smoky Pecans, page 85 or Sugared Pecans, page 263

CHOCOLATE CHUBBIES, PAGE 267

Goat Cheese With Marinated Roasted Peppers

Prep: 5 min.; **Grill:** 5 min.; **Stand:** 10 min.; **Chill:** 8 hr.

1 yellow bell pepper

1 red bell pepper

3 Anaheim chile peppers

3 Tbsp. olive oil

1 Tbsp. white wine vinegar

2 garlic cloves, pressed

1 (10.5-oz.) log goat cheese

French bread slices

1. Preheat oven to 350° to 400° (medium-high) heat. Grill peppers, without grill lid, over medium-high heat (350° to 400°), turning often, 5 to 7 minutes or until peppers look blistered.

2. Place peppers in a zip-top plastic freezer bag; seal and let stand 10 minutes to loosen skins. Peel peppers; remove and discard seeds. Chop peppers.

3. Combine peppers, oil, vinegar, and garlic; cover and chill at least 8 hours. Serve over goat cheese with bread slices. **Makes** 8 servings.

Spicy Southwestern Deviled Eggs

Prep: 15 min.; **Chill:** 1 hr.

1 dozen large eggs,
hard-cooked and peeled

6 Tbsp. mayonnaise

2 to 4 Tbsp. pickled sliced
jalapeño peppers, minced

1 Tbsp. yellow mustard

½ tsp. cumin

⅛ tsp. salt

Garnish: chopped fresh
cilantro

1. Cut eggs in half lengthwise, and carefully remove yolks. Mash yolks until smooth; stir in mayonnaise and next 4 ingredients. Spoon or pipe egg yolk mixture into egg whites. Cover and chill at least 1 hour or until ready to serve. Garnish, if desired. **Makes** 24 appetizers.

Buying tip: The fresher the eggs, the more difficult they can be to peel. For ease of peeling, buy and refrigerate your eggs 7 to 10 days before using.

Special Deviled Eggs

Prep: 15 min.

1 dozen large eggs,
hard-cooked and peeled

5 bacon slices, cooked
and crumbled

½ cup finely shredded Swiss
cheese

¼ cup plus 1 Tbsp.
mayonnaise

2½ Tbsp. cider vinegar

2 tsp. sugar

2 tsp. honey mustard

1½ tsp. freshly ground
pepper

¼ tsp. salt

Finely chopped green
onions or chives (optional)

1. Cut eggs in half lengthwise, and carefully remove yolks. Mash yolks until smooth. Add bacon and next 7 ingredients; stir until blended. Spoon yolk mixture evenly into egg whites. Sprinkle with green onions, if desired. **Makes** 24 appetizers.

tips for a tailgate

Deviled eggs are a welcome accompaniment with any tailgate. At any time of day, these bite-size morsels will work for brunch, as an appetizer, or a side dish. To perfectly cook the eggs, place eggs in a single layer in a saucepan with enough water to measure at least 1 inch above the eggs. Cover and bring to a boil. Remove eggs from heat and let stand, covered, in hot water 15 minutes. Drain and run under cold water or place in ice water to cool completely. Gently tap each shell and hold the egg under cold water as you peel off the shell.

Picnic Menu

Serves 8 to 10 hungry folks

CHAMPIONSHIP PORK BUTT, PAGE 49

Best BBQ Coleslaw

Baked Beans, page 250 or Spicy Baked Beans, page 251

BUNS OR BBQ BREAD

Best Barbecue Coleslaw

Prep: 13 min.; **Chill:** 2 hr.

2 (10-oz.) packages finely shredded cabbage

1 carrot, shredded

½ cup sugar

½ tsp. salt

⅛ tsp. pepper

½ cup mayonnaise

¼ cup milk

¼ cup buttermilk

2½ Tbsp. lemon juice

1½ Tbsp. white vinegar

1. Combine cabbage and carrot in a large bowl.
2. Whisk together sugar and next 7 ingredients until blended; toss with vegetables. Cover and chill at least 2 hours. **Makes** 8 to 10 servings.

Barbecue has endless possibilities when firing up the pit.

Cucumber-and-Tomato Salad

Prep: 15 min.; **Chill:** 3 hr.

2 cucumbers

1 large tomato

1 small green bell pepper

1 small red onion

⅓ cup vegetable oil

3 Tbsp. sugar

3 Tbsp. red wine vinegar

¾ tsp. salt

⅛ tsp. pepper

1. Cut cucumbers and tomato in half. Remove seeds. Chop cucumber, tomato, bell pepper, and onion.

2. Whisk together oil and next 4 ingredients in a large bowl until sugar dissolves. Add cucumber mixture, tossing to coat. Cover and chill 3 hours. **Makes** 3 to 4 servings.

Avocado Fruit Salad

You can prepare this salad a day ahead, but don't cut up the avocado or add garnishes until just before you serve it.

Prep: 15 min.; **Chill:** 1 hr.

1 (24-oz.) jar refrigerated orange and grapefruit sections, rinsed, drained, and patted dry

1 (24-oz.) jar refrigerated tropical mixed fruit in light syrup, rinsed, drained, and patted dry

2 cups cubed fresh cantaloupe

1 medium-size ripe avocado, halved and cut into chunks

¼ cup chopped fresh mint

2 Tbsp. lime juice

Garnishes: light sour cream, crushed pistachios

Shopping tip: We tested with Del Monte SunFresh Citrus Salad and Del Monte Sun-Fresh Tropical Mixed Fruit in Light Syrup With Passion Fruit Juice.

1. Toss together first 6 ingredients. Cover and chill 1 hour. Garnish, if desired. **Makes** 6 to 8 servings.

Barbecue Scalloped Potatoes

Prep: 15 min.; **Cook:** 30 min.; **Bake:** 45 min.

3 large baking potatoes
(about 2½ lb.)

1½ tsp. salt, divided

1 (10¾-oz.) can cream of
mushroom soup, undiluted

1 (5-oz.) can evaporated milk

¼ cup spicy barbecue sauce

¼ tsp. onion salt

2 cups shredded sharp
Cheddar cheese

⅛ tsp. paprika

1. Preheat oven to 350°.
2. Cook potatoes with 1 tsp. salt in boiling water to cover 30 to 40 minutes or just until tender. Let cool slightly; peel and slice. Set aside.
3. Stir together remaining ½ tsp. salt, soup, and next 3 ingredients until blended.
4. Layer half each of potato slices, barbecue sauce mixture, and cheese in a lightly greased 2-qt. round baking dish. Repeat layers; sprinkle top evenly with paprika.
5. Bake at 350° for 45 minutes or until golden. **Makes** 6 servings.

4th of July Menu

Serves 4 hungry folks

BACON-WRAPPED BARBECUE BURGERS, PAGE 113

Potato Salad With Sweet Pickles

Southern Sweet Tea, page 204

Blackberry Cobbler, page 268

Potato Salad With Sweet Pickles

Prep: 20 min.; **Cook:** 40 min.; **Cool:** 10 min.

1 (4-lb.) bag large baking potatoes

2½ tsp. salt, divided

1 cup mayonnaise

1 Tbsp. spicy brown mustard

¾ tsp. pepper

3 hard-cooked eggs, grated

⅓ cup sweet salad cube pickles

Garnish: chopped fresh parsley

1. Cook potatoes in boiling water to cover and salted with 1 tsp. salt 40 minutes or until tender; drain and cool 10 to 15 minutes.

2. Stir together mayonnaise, mustard, pepper, and remaining 1½ tsp. salt in a large bowl.

3. Peel potatoes, and cut into 1-inch cubes. Add warm potato cubes, grated eggs, and pickles to bowl, and gently toss with mayonnaise mixture. Garnish, if desired. Serve immediately, or, if desired, cover and chill. **Makes** 8 to 10 servings.

Time-saving tip: To reduce cooking time, use 4 extra-large baking potatoes (about 1 pound each), peeled and cut into 1-inch cubes. Proceed as directed, reducing cooking time to 20 minutes or until tender. Drain and cool 10 minutes. Increase mayonnaise to 1½ cups, and proceed as directed.

Grilled Potato Salad

Prep: 20 min.; **Cook:** 8 min. per batch; **Grill:** 30 min.

8 bacon slices

4 medium-size red potatoes, cut into ¾-inch cubes (about 5 cups cubed)

1 large white onion, cut into ½-inch-thick strips

Potato Salad Dry Rub

Potato Salad Dressing

1. Preheat grill to 350° to 400° (medium-high) heat. Cook bacon, in batches, in a large skillet over medium-high heat 8 to 10 minutes or until crisp; remove bacon, and drain on paper towels, reserving drippings in skillet. Crumble bacon.

2. Add potatoes, onion, and Potato Salad Dry Rub to hot drippings in skillet, tossing to coat. Remove potato mixture with a slotted spoon.

3. Grill potato mixture, covered with grill lid, in a grill wok or metal basket 30 minutes or until tender, stirring every 5 minutes. Transfer mixture to a large bowl. Add Potato Salad Dressing, and toss to coat. Stir in bacon. Serve warm. **Makes** 4 to 5 servings.

Potato Salad Dry Rub

Prep: 5 min.

2 tsp. salt

1¼ tsp. pepper

1 tsp. paprika

1 tsp. garlic powder

¼ tsp. dried thyme

¼ tsp. dried crushed rosemary

⅛ tsp. celery seeds

1. Stir together all ingredients. Store in an airtight container up to 1 month. **Makes** about 2 Tbsp.

Potato Salad Dressing

Prep: 5 min.

5½ Tbsp. mayonnaise

2 Tbsp. Dijon mustard

2 tsp. Worcestershire sauce

1. Stir together all ingredients. Store in an airtight container in refrigerator up to 2 weeks. **Makes** about ½ cup.

Georgia

Here's where to get great 'Q in the state.

Smokejack Southern Grill & BBQ

29 South Main Street
Alpharetta
(770) 410-7611
www.smokejackbbq.com

Fat Matt's Rib Shack

1811 Piedmont Avenue NE.
Atlanta
(404) 607-1622
www.fatmattsribshack.com

ROLLING BONES PREMIUM PIT BBQ

377 Edgewood Avenue
Atlanta
(404) 222-2324
www.rollingbonesbbq.com

Maddy's Ribs & Blues

1479 Scott Blvd.
Decatur
(404) 377-0301
www.maddysribs.com

Poole's Bar-B-Q

164 Craig Street
East Ellijay
(706) 635-4100
www.poolesbarbq.com

OLD CLINTON BAR-B-Q

4214 Gray Highway
Gray
(478) 986-3225
www.oldclintonbbq.com

FRESH AIR BAR-B-QUE

1164 State 42 South
Jackson (Flovilla)
(770) 775-3182
www.freshairbarbecue.com

Sprayberry's Barbecue

229 Jackson Street
Newnan
(770) 253-4421
www.sprayberrysbbq.com

JOHNNY HARRIS RESTAURANT & BBQ SAUCE COMPANY

1651 East Victory Drive
Savannah
(912) 354-7810 or (888) 547-2823
www.johnnyharris.com

Garlic Mashed Potatoes

Prep: 20 min.; **Cook:** 30 min.

8 baking potatoes, peeled and quartered (about 4 lb.)

1¾ tsp. salt, divided

½ cup butter, softened

¾ cup half-and-half

3 large garlic cloves, pressed

½ tsp. ground white pepper

¼ cup chopped fresh parsley

1. Bring potatoes, 1 tsp. salt, and water to cover to a boil in a Dutch oven or stockpot; cover, reduce heat, and simmer 30 minutes or until tender. Drain.
2. Beat potatoes, remaining ¾ tsp. salt, butter, half-and-half, garlic, and white pepper at medium speed with an electric mixer until smooth. Stir in parsley. **Makes** 8 servings.

Smoked Gouda Grits

Buy a 7-oz. wheel of smoked Gouda cheese to get the right amount.

Prep: 5 min.; **Cook:** 5 min.

6 cups low-sodium chicken broth or water

2 cups milk

1 tsp. salt

½ tsp. ground white pepper

2 cups uncooked quick-cooking grits

1⅔ cups shredded smoked Gouda cheese

3 Tbsp. unsalted butter

1. Bring first 4 ingredients to a boil in a medium saucepan; gradually whisk in grits. Cover, reduce heat, and simmer, stirring occasionally, 5 minutes or until thickened. Add cheese and butter, stirring until melted. **Makes** 6 to 8 servings.

Baked Beans

Prep: 15 min.; **Cook:** 11 min.; **Bake:** 45 min.

4 bacon slices

1 small onion, diced

4 (15-oz.) cans pork and beans in tomato sauce, drained

⅓ cup firmly packed brown sugar

½ cup ketchup

½ cup sorghum syrup or molasses

1½ tsp. Worcestershire sauce

1 tsp. dry mustard

1. Preheat oven to 350°. Cook bacon in a skillet over medium-high heat 4 minutes; drain, reserving 1 tsp. drippings in skillet. Set bacon aside.
2. Sauté onion in hot bacon drippings 7 minutes or until tender. Stir together onions, pork and beans, and next 5 ingredients in a lightly greased 11- x 7-inch baking dish. Top bean mixture with bacon.
3. Bake at 350° for 45 minutes or until bubbly. **Makes** 6 to 8 servings.

Spicy Baked Beans

Prep: 15 min.; **Cook:** 10 min.; **Bake:** 45 min.

1 lb. ground pork sausage

1 onion, chopped

2 (28-oz.) cans bold-and-spicy baked beans

1 (15-oz.) can black beans, drained

1 (15-oz.) can light or dark kidney beans, drained

3 cups bottled barbecue sauce

½ cup firmly packed dark brown sugar

¼ cup yellow mustard

1 tsp. black pepper

½ tsp. ground red pepper

1 tsp. garlic powder (optional)

1. Preheat oven to 350°. Cook pork sausage in an ovenproof Dutch oven over medium-high heat, stirring until sausage crumbles and is no longer pink. Drain, reserving 2 tsp. drippings in Dutch oven. Return sausage to Dutch oven, and stir in onion, next 8 ingredients, and, if desired, garlic powder.

2. Bake at 350° for 45 minutes or until thickened and bubbly. **Makes** 12 servings.

Fried Green Tomatoes With Bread-and-Butter Pickle Rémoulade

Prep: 15 min.; **Fry:** 4 min. per batch

4 large green tomatoes

2 tsp. salt

1 tsp. pepper

1½ cups buttermilk

1 cup plain white cornmeal

1 Tbsp. Creole seasoning

2 cups all-purpose flour, divided

Vegetable or peanut oil

Salt to taste

Bread-and-Butter Pickle Rémoulade

1. Preheat oven to 200°. Cut tomatoes into ¼-inch-thick slices. Sprinkle both sides of tomatoes evenly with salt and pepper.

2. Pour buttermilk into a shallow dish or pie plate. Stir together cornmeal, Creole seasoning, and 1 cup flour in another shallow dish or pie plate.

3. Dredge tomatoes in remaining 1 cup flour. Dip tomatoes in buttermilk, and dredge in cornmeal mixture.

4. Pour oil to a depth of 2 inches in a large cast-iron skillet; heat over medium heat to 350°. Fry tomatoes, in batches, 2 to 3 minutes on each side or until golden. Drain on paper towels. Transfer to a wire rack; keep warm in a 200° oven until ready to serve. Sprinkle with salt to taste. Serve with Bread-and-Butter Pickle Rémoulade. **Makes** 6 to 8 servings.

Bread-and-Butter Pickle Rémoulade

Prep: 15 min.

¾ cup mayonnaise

¼ cup Creole mustard

1 Tbsp. chopped fresh chives

1 Tbsp. chopped fresh parsley

1 Tbsp. finely chopped bread-and-butter pickles

1 tsp. lemon zest

1 Tbsp. lemon juice

½ tsp. hot sauce

¼ tsp. filé powder

⅛ tsp. salt

⅛ tsp. pepper

1. Stir together all ingredients. **Makes** about 1 cup.

Storage tip: This will keep in the refrigerator for about a week. Serve any leftovers on sandwiches or with boiled shrimp.

To lighten: Substitute ¾ cup light mayonnaise for regular mayonnaise.

Grilled Okra and Tomato Skewers

Prep: 12 min.; **Soak:** 30 min.; **Grill:** 6 min.

8 (12-inch) wooden or metal skewers

2 small onions, each cut into 8 wedges

24 okra pods (about ¾ lb.), trimmed

16 cherry tomatoes (about ½ lb.)

4 tsp. olive oil

1 tsp. kosher salt

1 tsp. freshly ground black pepper

1 tsp. water

½ tsp. ground red pepper

⅛ tsp. sugar

2 garlic cloves, minced

1. Preheat grill to 350° to 400° (medium-high) heat. If using wooden skewers, soak in water 30 minutes.

2. Divide each onion wedge into 2 equal pieces. Thread 3 okra pods, 2 cherry tomatoes, and 2 onion pieces alternately onto each of 8 (12-inch) skewers. Combine olive oil, kosher salt, and remaining ingredients in a small bowl, stirring with a whisk. Brush olive oil mixture over skewers. Place skewers on a grill rack coated with cooking spray, and grill, uncovered, for 3 minutes on each side or until tender. **Makes** 8 servings.

Make-ahead tip: Assemble skewers the night before; brush them with the oil mixture before grilling. Flavor oil mixture with dried ground herbs to suit your taste. Look for okra pods of similar size to assure even grilling.

USA Barbecue Championship

Hot Springs, Arkansas

The total purse for all winners is $100,000 in this noteworthy cook-off.

What is it?

The world's richest barbecue competition for pros and amateurs, plus entertainment and events for the entire family.

What is there to do?

• Stroll through the vintage motorcycle and classic car show
• Glance to the sky to see a collection of commemorative airplanes from World War II.
• Purchase a taste kit and sample several of the competitors' creations

Who hosts it?

The USA Barbecue Championship is presented by Smoke on the Water Productions, Inc. It is sanctioned by the Kansas City Barbecue Society.

How do I get more information?

Visit www.smokeonthewaterbbq.com or call (870) 536-8175.

Photos courtesy of Smoke on the Water Productions, Inc.

Grilled Artichokes and Asparagus

You can prep Steps 1 and 2 the day before and place artichokes in zip-top plastic bags in the refrigerator. The choke is the inedible prickly center of the artichoke you scoop out after boiling in water.

Prep: 15 min.; **Cook:** 25 min.; **Grill:** 15 min. (artichokes), 3 min. (asparagus)

4 fresh artichokes

2 lb. fresh asparagus

½ cup olive oil

¼ cup fresh lemon juice

½ tsp. salt

½ tsp. freshly ground pepper

Garnish: lemon wedges

1. Preheat grill to 350° to 400° (medium-high) heat. Wash artichokes by plunging up and down in cold water. Cut off stem ends, and trim about 1 inch from top of each artichoke. Remove and discard any loose bottom leaves. Trim and discard one-fourth off top of each outer leaf with scissors.

2. Bring artichokes and water to cover to a boil in a Dutch oven; cover, reduce heat, and simmer 25 minutes. Drain; pat dry with paper towels.

3. Cut artichokes in half lengthwise. Remove choke using a small spoon or melon baller. Snap off and discard tough ends of asparagus.

4. Stir together olive oil and next 3 ingredients. Brush cut sides of artichoke halves with one-third of olive oil mixture. Brush asparagus evenly with one-third of olive oil mixture, reserving remaining olive oil mixture for later use.

5. Grill artichokes, covered with grill lid, cut sides down, 10 minutes; turn and grill 5 more minutes. Grill asparagus, covered, 1 to 2 minutes; turn and grill 2 more minutes or until tender. Garnish, if desired. Drizzle with reserved olive oil mixture, if desired, and serve immediately. **Makes** 8 servings.

tools of the trade

Aluminum Foil and Pans: Heavy-duty foil makes a handy container for smaller grilled food like veggies or shrimp when you don't want to bother with skewers or a grill basket. Disposable aluminum pans are perfect for holding wood chips or creating your own water box when cooking with indirect heat.

Roasted Camp Corn

Serve with additional sweet pepper sauce and Creole seasoning, if desired.

Prep: 30 min.; **Grill:** 24 min.

6 ears fresh yellow corn with husks

¼ cup butter

1 tsp. dried basil

1 tsp. sweet pepper sauce

½ tsp. Creole seasoning

¼ tsp. black pepper

Shopping tip: We tested with Pickapeppa Sauce for sweet pepper sauce.

1. Preheat grill to 400° to 500° (high) heat. Remove heavy outer husks from corn; pull back (but do not remove) inner husks. Remove and discard silks; rinse corn, and dry with paper towels. Set aside.

2. Melt ¼ cup butter in a small saucepan over low heat. Stir in 1 tsp. basil and next 3 ingredients, stirring until blended.

3. Brush corn evenly with butter mixture. Pull husks back over corn.

4. Grill corn, covered with grill lid, 24 minutes, making quarter turns every 6 to 7 minutes. Pull back husks before serving. **Makes** 6 servings.

Cream-Filled Grilled Pound Cake

We didn't think pound cake could get any better until we grilled it. Choose homemade, frozen, or fresh store-bought cake.

Prep: 5 min.; **Grill:** 4 min.

4 Tbsp. pineapple cream cheese

8 (½-inch-thick) slices pound cake

Sweetened whipped cream

Fresh strawberries and blueberries

1. Preheat grill to 350° to 400° (medium-high) heat. Spread pineapple cream cheese evenly over 1 side of 4 pound cake slices. Top with remaining 4 pound cake slices.

2. Grill, covered with grill lid, 2 to 3 minutes on each side. Top with whipped cream and berries. Serve immediately. **Makes** 4 servings.

You can throw side dishes and even desserts on the grill to round out the meal.

Praline Bundt Cake

Prep: 30 min.; **Bake:** 1 hr., 20 min.; **Cool:** 1 hr.

1 cup chopped pecans

1 cup butter, softened

1 (8-oz.) package cream cheese, softened

1 (16-oz.) package dark brown sugar

4 large eggs

2½ cups all-purpose flour

1 tsp. baking powder

½ tsp. baking soda

¼ tsp. salt

1 (8-oz.) container sour cream

2 tsp. vanilla extract

Praline Icing

Sugared Pecans (opposite page)

1. Preheat oven to 350°. Arrange 1 cup pecans in a single layer on a baking sheet. Bake at 350° for 5 to 7 minutes or until toasted. Cool on a wire rack 15 minutes or until completely cool. Reduce oven temperature to 325°.
2. Beat butter and cream cheese at medium speed with an electric mixer until creamy. Gradually add brown sugar, beating until well blended. Add eggs, 1 at a time, beating just until blended after each addition.
3. Sift together 2½ cups flour and next 3 ingredients. Add to butter mixture alternately with sour cream, beginning and ending with flour mixture. Beat batter at low speed just until blended after each addition. Stir in toasted pecans and vanilla. Spoon batter into a greased and floured 12-cup Bundt pan.
4. Bake at 325° for 1 hour and 15 minutes or until a long wooden pick inserted in center comes out clean. Cool cake in pan on a wire rack 15 minutes; remove from pan to wire rack, and let cool 30 minutes or until completely cool.
5. Prepare Praline Icing, and spoon immediately over cake. Sprinkle top of cake with Sugared Pecans. **Makes** 12 servings.

Praline Icing

Prep: 10 min.; **Cook:** 4 min.

1 cup firmly packed light brown sugar

½ cup butter

¼ cup milk

1 cup powdered sugar, sifted

1 tsp. vanilla extract

1. Bring first 3 ingredients to a boil in a 2-qt. saucepan over medium heat, whisking constantly; boil 1 minute. Remove from heat; whisk in powdered sugar and vanilla until smooth. Stir gently 3 to 5 minutes or until mixture begins to cool and thickens slightly. Use immediately. **Makes** about 1½ cups.

Sugared Pecans

Prep: 10 min.; **Bake:** 18 min.; **Cool:** 30 min.

1 egg white

4 cups pecan halves
(about 1 lb.)

⅓ cup granulated sugar

⅓ cup firmly packed light
brown sugar

1. Preheat oven to 350°. Whisk egg white until foamy; add pecans, and stir until evenly coated.

2. Stir together sugars; sprinkle over pecans. Stir gently until pecans are evenly coated. Spread pecans in a single layer in a lightly greased aluminum foil-lined 15- x 10-inch jelly-roll pan.

3. Bake at 350° for 18 to 20 minutes or until pecans are toasted and dry, stirring once after 10 minutes. Remove from oven, and let cool 30 minutes or until completely cool. **Makes** about 5 cups.

Storage tip: Store pecans in a zip-top plastic freezer bag at room temperature up to 3 days or freeze up to 3 weeks.

Chocolate Marble Sheet Cake

Prep: 20 min.; **Bake:** 23 min.; **Cool:** 1 hr.

1 cup butter, softened

1¾ cups sugar, divided

2 large eggs

2 tsp. vanilla extract

2½ cups all-purpose flour

1 Tbsp. baking powder

½ tsp. salt

1 cup half-and-half

¼ cup unsweetened cocoa

3 Tbsp. hot water

Mocha Frosting

1. Preheat oven to 325°. Beat butter and 1½ cups sugar at medium speed with a heavy-duty electric stand mixer 4 to 5 minutes or until creamy. Add eggs, 1 at a time, beating just until blended after each addition. Beat in vanilla.

2. Sift together flour, baking powder, and salt. Add to butter mixture alternately with half-and-half, beginning and ending with flour mixture. Beat at low speed just until blended after each addition, stopping to scrape bowl as needed.

3. Spoon 1¼ cups batter into a 2-qt. bowl, and stir in cocoa, 3 Tbsp. hot water, and remaining ¼ cup sugar until well blended.

4. Spread remaining vanilla batter into a greased and floured 15- x 10-inch jelly-roll pan. Spoon chocolate batter onto vanilla batter in pan; gently swirl with a knife or small spatula.

5. Bake at 325° for 23 to 28 minutes or until a wooden pick inserted in center comes out clean. Cool completely in pan on a wire rack (about 1 hour). Spread top of cake with Mocha Frosting. **Makes** 12 servings.

Mocha Frosting

Prep: 10 min.

3 cups powdered sugar

⅔ cup unsweetened cocoa

3 Tbsp. hot brewed coffee

2 tsp. vanilla extract

½ cup butter, softened

3 to 4 Tbsp. half-and-half

1. Whisk together sugar and cocoa. Combine coffee and vanilla.

2. Beat butter at medium speed with a heavy-duty electric stand mixer until creamy; gradually add sugar mixture alternately with coffee mixture, beating at low speed until blended. Beat in half-and-half, 1 Tbsp. at a time, until smooth and mixture reaches desired spreading consistency. **Makes** 2⅓ cups.

Caramel-Pecan Bars

Prep: 20 min.; **Bake:** 45 min.; **Cool:** 1 hr.; **Cook:** 5 min.

3½ cups coarsely chopped pecans

2 cups all-purpose flour

⅔ cup powdered sugar

¾ cup butter, cubed

½ cup firmly packed brown sugar

½ cup honey

⅔ cup butter

3 Tbsp. whipping cream

1. Preheat oven to 350°. Arrange pecans in a single layer on a baking sheet. Bake at 350° for 5 to 7 minutes or until lightly toasted. Cool on a wire rack 15 minutes or until completely cool.

2. Pulse flour, powdered sugar, and ¾ cup butter in a food processor 5 to 6 times or until mixture resembles coarse meal. Press crumb mixture evenly on bottom and ¾ inch up sides of a lightly greased heavy-duty aluminum foil-lined 13- x 9-inch pan.

3. Bake at 350° for 20 minutes or until edges are lightly browned. Cool on a wire rack 15 minutes or until completely cool.

4. Bring brown sugar, honey, ⅔ cup butter, and whipping cream to a boil in a 3-qt. saucepan over medium-high heat. Stir in toasted pecans, and spoon hot filling into prepared crust.

5. Bake at 350° for 25 to 30 minutes or until golden and bubbly. Cool on a wire rack 30 minutes or until completely cool. When completely cool, using the aluminum foil as handles, carefully lift from the pan, and transfer to a serving tray. Cut into squares. **Makes** 12 servings.

Chocolate Chubbies

Prep: 20 min.; **Bake:** 12 min. per batch

6 (1-oz.) semisweet chocolate squares, chopped

2 (1-oz.) unsweetened chocolate squares, chopped

⅓ cup butter

3 large eggs

1 cup sugar

¼ cup all-purpose flour

½ tsp. baking powder

⅛ tsp. salt

2 cups (12 oz.) semisweet chocolate morsels

2 cups coarsely chopped pecans

2 cups coarsely chopped walnuts

1. Preheat oven to 325°. Combine first 3 ingredients in a heavy saucepan; cook, stirring often, over low heat until chocolate melts. Remove from heat; cool slightly.

2. Beat eggs and sugar at medium speed with an electric mixer until smooth; add chocolate mixture, beating well.

3. Combine flour, baking powder, and salt; add to chocolate mixture, stirring just until dry ingredients are moistened. Fold in chocolate morsels, pecans, and walnuts.

4. Drop batter by teaspoonfuls 2 inches apart onto lightly greased baking sheets.

5. Bake at 325° for 12 to 15 minutes or until done. Cool cookies on baking sheet 1 minute. Remove to wire racks; cool. **Makes** 3½ dozen.

Blackberry Cobbler

Prep: 10 min.; **Bake:** 45 min.

1⅓ cups sugar

½ cup all-purpose flour

½ cup butter, melted

2 tsp. vanilla extract

2 (14-oz.) bags frozen blackberries, thawed

½ (15-oz.) package refrigerated piecrusts

1 Tbsp. sugar

Vanilla ice cream (optional)

Sugared Piecrust Sticks (optional)

1. Preheat oven to 425°. Stir together first 4 ingredients in a large bowl. Gently stir in blackberries until sugar mixture is crumbly. Spoon fruit mixture into a lightly greased 11- x 7-inch baking dish.

2. Cut 1 piecrust into ½-inch-wide strips, and arrange strips diagonally over blackberry mixture. Sprinkle top with 1 Tbsp. sugar.

3. Bake at 425° for 45 minutes or until crust is golden brown and center is bubbly. Serve with ice cream and Sugared Piecrust Sticks, if desired. **Makes** 6 to 8 servings.

Sugared Piecrust Sticks

Prep: 10 min.; **Bake:** 6 min.

½ (15-oz.) package refrigerated piecrusts

1 Tbsp. sugar

1. Preheat oven to 425°. Cut 1 refrigerated piecrust into ½-inch-thick strips. Sprinkle strips with sugar; place on a lightly greased baking sheet. Bake at 425° for 6 to 8 minutes or until golden brown. **Makes** 6 to 8 servings.

Texas

Here's where to get great 'Q in the state.

STUBB'S BAR-B-QUE
801 Red River Street
Austin
(512) 480-8341
www.stubbsaustin.com

The Salt Lick
18300 FM 1826
Driftwood
(512) 858-4959
www.saltlickbbq.com

Meyer's Elgin Smokehouse
188 U.S. 290 East
Elgin
(512) 281-3331
www.meyerselginsausage.com

Capital Q Texan BBQ
1228 Seawall Boulevard
Galveston
(409) 974-4585
www.capitalqbbq.com

COUNTRY TAVERN
State 31 and FM 2767
Kilgore
(903) 984-9954
www.countrytavern.com

COOPER'S OLD TIME PIT BAR-B-QUE
604 West Young
Llano
(325) 247-5713
www.coopersbbq.com

Black's Barbecue
215 North Main Street
Lockhart
(512) 398-2712
www.blacksbbq.com

KREUZ MARKET
619 North Colorado Street
Lockhart
(512) 398-2361
www.kreuzmarket.com

LOUIE MUELLER BARBECUE
206 West Second Street
Taylor
(512) 352-6206
www.louiemueller
barbecue.com

Clem Mikeska's Bar-B-Q
1217 South 57th Street
Temple
(254) 778-5481
www.clembbq.com

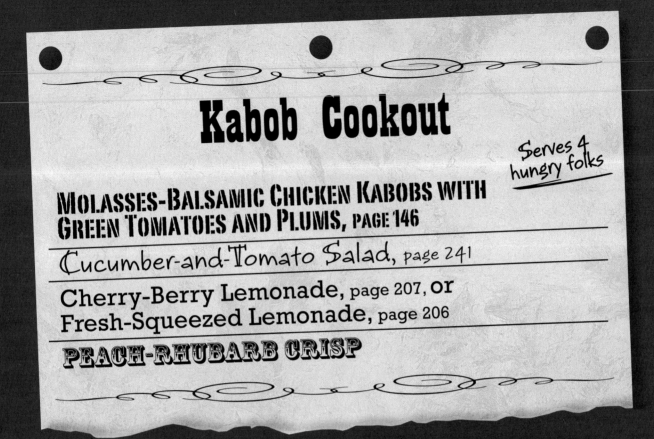

Kabob Cookout

Serves 4 hungry folks

Molasses-Balsamic Chicken Kabobs with Green Tomatoes and Plums, page 146

Cucumber-and-Tomato Salad, page 241

Cherry-Berry Lemonade, page 207, **or** Fresh-Squeezed Lemonade, page 206

PEACH-RHUBARB CRISP

Peach-Rhubarb Crisp

Prep: 15 min.; **Bake:** 45 min.

1 (20-oz.) bag frozen peaches, thawed

2 (16-oz.) packages frozen sliced rhubarb, thawed

1½ cups granulated sugar

3 Tbsp. lemon juice

1¼ cups all-purpose flour, divided

⅓ cup uncooked quick-cooking oats

⅓ cup firmly packed brown sugar

⅓ cup cold butter, cut into small pieces

Vanilla ice cream

1. Preheat oven to 375°. Combine first 4 ingredients in a medium bowl; add ¼ cup flour, stirring well. Pour mixture into a 13- x-9-inch baking dish coated with cooking spray.
2. Combine oats, brown sugar, and remaining 1 cup flour in a small bowl; cut in cold butter with a fork or pastry blender until mixture resembles coarse crumbs. Sprinkle mixture evenly over fruit filling.
3. Bake at 375° for 45 to 50 minutes or until bubbly. Serve with ice cream. **Makes** 10 servings.

Georgia Peach Trifle

Prep: 15 min.; **Chill:** 2 hr., 5 min.

1 (3.4-oz.) package vanilla instant pudding mix

2 cups milk

6 large fresh peaches, peeled and sliced

3 Tbsp. granulated sugar

½ (20-oz.) package pound cake

⅓ cup bourbon, divided

1 cup whipping cream

2 Tbsp. powdered sugar

½ cup sliced almonds, toasted

1. Prepare pudding mix according to package directions, using 2 cups milk. Cover and chill 5 minutes.

2. Toss sliced peaches with granulated sugar.

3. Cut pound cake into ½-inch slices. Place half of cake slices on bottom of a trifle dish or deep bowl; drizzle evenly with half of bourbon. Spoon half of peach mixture evenly over cake slices. Spread half of pudding over peaches. Repeat with remaining cake slices, bourbon, peach mixture, and pudding. Cover and chill at least 2 hours.

4. Beat whipping cream at medium speed with an electric mixer until foamy; gradually add powdered sugar, beating until soft peaks form. Spread whipped cream over trifle; sprinkle with almonds. **Makes** 8 servings.

Lemony Ice-Cream Pie

Prep: 10 min.; **Freeze:** 2 hr.

1 qt. vanilla ice cream, softened

1 (6-oz.) can frozen lemonade concentrate, partially thawed

1 (9-inch) graham cracker crust

Garnishes: fresh raspberries, lemon slices, fresh mint sprigs

1. Stir together ice cream and lemonade concentrate until blended. Spoon into crust, and freeze 2 hours or until firm. Garnish, if desired. **Makes** 8 servings.

Vanilla-Cinnamon Ice Cream

While this delicious ice cream contains no fat, it's not a low-calorie dessert.

Prep: 1 hr.

2 (14-oz.) cans fat-free
sweetened condensed milk

1 qt. fat-free half-and-half

1 Tbsp. vanilla extract

1 tsp. ground cinnamon

1. Stir together all ingredients, and pour into freezer container of a 1-gal. electric ice-cream freezer.
2. Freeze according to manufacturer's instructions. Serve immediately, or place in freezer. **Makes** 7½ cups.

Grilled Pineapple With Vanilla-Cinnamon Ice Cream

Prep: 15 min.; Grill: 10 min.

1 fresh pineapple

3 Tbsp. brown sugar

½ tsp. ground cinnamon

1 Tbsp. grated fresh ginger

Vanilla-Cinnamon Ice Cream

1. Cut pineapple lengthwise into quarters; discard core. Remove pineapple pulp, discarding shell.
2. Combine brown sugar and cinnamon. Sprinkle evenly over pineapple pulp. Sprinkle evenly with ginger.
3. Preheat grill to 350° to 400° (medium-high) heat. Coat a food rack with cooking spray; place on grill. Place pineapple on rack, and grill, covered with grill lid, 5 to 7 minutes on each side. Remove pineapple from grill, and cut into chunks. Serve with Vanilla-Cinnamon Ice Cream. **Makes** 6 servings.

Substitution tip: Low-fat or fat-free vanilla frozen yogurt may be substituted for Vanilla-Cinnamon Ice Cream.

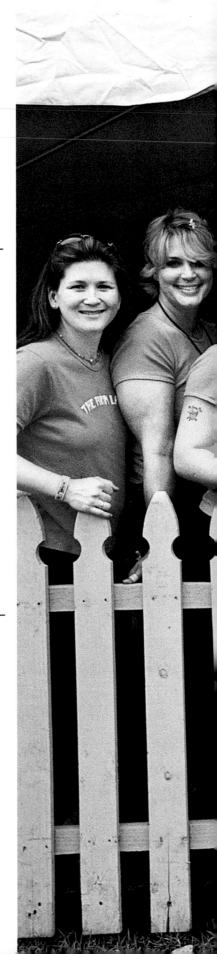

Refreshing Lime Sherbet

Be careful not to remove any of the white pith underneath when grating the zest, or your sherbet will taste bitter.

Prep: 15 min.; **Freeze:** about 35 min.

4 tsp. finely grated lime zest (about 1 large lime)

1 cup sugar

3 cups half-and-half

½ cup fresh lime juice (about 4 limes)

½ cup water

⅛ tsp. salt

1. Stir together all ingredients in a large bowl, stirring until well blended.

2. Pour lime mixture into freezer container of a 4-qt. electric ice-cream maker; freeze according to manufacturer's instructions. **Makes** 5 cups.

Refreshing Lemon Sherbet: Substitute a large lemon for the lime and fresh lemon juice for lime juice. Proceed as directed.

Nutter Butter®–Banana Pudding Trifle

This homemade pudding is divine, economical, and uses on-hand ingredients. The pudding has thickened enough when a distinct trail is left in the mixture when you stir with a spoon. The cookies will soften the longer the dessert chills.

Prep: 35 min.; **Cook:** 15 min.; **Stand:** 30 min.; **Chill:** 2 hr.

3 cups milk

3 large eggs

¾ cup sugar

⅓ cup all-purpose flour

2 Tbsp. butter

2 tsp. vanilla extract

5 medium-size ripe bananas

1 (1-lb.) package peanut butter sandwich cookies

2 cups sweetened whipped cream

Garnishes: peanut butter sandwich cookies, dried banana chips, fresh mint sprigs

Shopping tip: We tested with Jell-O Vanilla Instant Pudding and Pie Filling, Cool Whip Extra Creamy, and Nabisco Nutter Butter Sandwich Cookies.

1. Whisk together first 4 ingredients in a large saucepan over medium-low heat. Cook, whisking constantly, 15 to 20 minutes or until thickened. Remove from heat; stir in butter and vanilla until butter is melted.
2. Fill a large bowl with ice. Place saucepan in ice, and let stand, stirring occasionally, 30 minutes or until mixture is thoroughly chilled.
3. Meanwhile, cut bananas into ¼-inch slices. Break cookies into thirds.
4. Spoon half of pudding mixture into a 3-qt. bowl or smaller separate bowls. Top with bananas and cookies. Spoon remaining pudding mixture over bananas and cookies. Top with sweetened whipped cream. Cover and chill 2 to 24 hours. Garnish, if desired. **Makes** 8 to 10 servings.

Nutter Butter®-Banana Pudding Trifle: Omit eggs, sugar, flour, and butter. Substitute thawed extra creamy whipped topping for sweetened whipped cream. Reduce vanilla to 1 tsp. Place 3 cups milk and vanilla in large bowl; add 2 (3.4-oz.) packages vanilla instant pudding mix. Beat with an electric mixer at medium speed 2 minutes or until thickened; let stand 5 minutes. Stir in 1 (8-oz.) container sour cream. Proceed with recipe as directed in Steps 2 through 4.

metric equivalents

The recipes that appear in this cookbook use the standard U.S. method for measuring liquid and dry or solid ingredients (teaspoons, tablespoons, and cups). The information in the following charts is provided to help cooks outside the United States successfully use these recipes. All equivalents are approximate.

Metric Equivalents for Different Types of Ingredients

A standard cup measure of a dry or solid ingredient will vary in weight depending on the type of ingredient. A standard cup of liquid is the same volume for any type of liquid. Use the following chart when converting standard cup measures to grams (weight) or milliliters (volume).

Standard Cup	Fine Powder (ex. flour)	Grain (ex. rice)	Granular (ex. sugar)	Liquid Solids (ex. butter)	Liquid (ex. milk)
1	140 g	150 g	190 g	200 g	240 ml
¾	105 g	113 g	143 g	150 g	180 ml
⅔	93 g	100 g	125 g	133 g	160 ml
½	70 g	75 g	95 g	100 g	120 ml
⅓	47 g	50 g	63 g	67 g	80 ml
¼	35 g	38 g	48 g	50 g	60 ml
⅛	18 g	19 g	24 g	25 g	30 ml

Useful Equivalents for Liquid Ingredients by Volume

¼ tsp			=	1 ml
½ tsp			=	2 ml
1 tsp			=	5 ml
3 tsp = 1 Tbsp		= ½ fl oz	=	15 ml
2 Tbsp	= ⅛ cup	= 1 fl oz	=	30 ml
4 Tbsp	= ¼ cup	= 2 fl oz	=	60 ml
5⅓ Tbsp	= ⅓ cup	= 3 fl oz	=	80 ml
8 Tbsp	= ½ cup	= 4 fl oz	=	120 ml
10⅔ Tbsp	= ⅔ cup	= 5 fl oz	=	160 ml
12 Tbsp	= ¾ cup	= 6 fl oz	=	180 ml
16 Tbsp	= 1 cup	= 8 fl oz	=	240 ml
1 pt	= 2 cups	= 16 fl oz	=	480 ml
1 qt	= 4 cups	= 32 fl oz	=	960 ml
		33 fl oz	=	1000 ml = 1 l

Useful Equivalents for Dry Ingredients by Weight

(To convert ounces to grams, multiply the number of ounces by 30.)

1 oz	=	¹⁄₁₆ lb	=	30 g
4 oz	=	¼ lb	=	120 g
8 oz	=	½ lb	=	240 g
12 oz	=	¾ lb	=	360 g
16 oz	=	1 lb	=	480 g

Useful Equivalents for Length

(To convert inches to centimeters, multiply the number of inches by 2.5.)

1 in		=	2.5 cm	
6 in	= ½ ft	=	15 cm	
12 in	= 1 ft	=	30 cm	
36 in	= 3 ft = 1 yd	=	90 cm	
40 in		=	100 cm	= 1 m

Useful Equivalents for Cooking/Oven Temperatures

	Fahrenheit	Celsius	Gas Mark
Freeze water	32° F	0° C	
Room temperature	68° F	20° C	
Boil water	212° F	100° C	
Bake	325° F	160° C	3
	350° F	180° C	4
	375° F	190° C	5
	400° F	200° C	6
	425° F	220° C	7
	450° F	230° C	8
Broil			Grill

index

Recipes are listed in regular type;
tips, menus, and other special features are italicized.